New Directions for
Student Services

Elizabeth J. Whitt
EDITOR-IN-CHIEF

John H. Schuh
ASSOCIATE EDITOR

Facilitating the Moral Growth of College Students

Debora L. Liddell
and Diane L. Cooper
EDITORS

Number 139 • Fall 2012
Jossey-Bass
San Francisco

FACILITATING THE MORAL GROWTH OF COLLEGE STUDENTS
Debora L. Liddell and Diane L. Cooper (eds.)
New Directions for Student Services, no. 139
Elizabeth J. Whitt, Editor-in-Chief
John H. Schuh, Associate Editor

NEW DIRECTIONS FOR STUDENT SERVICES (ISSN 0164-7970, e-ISSN 1536-0695) is part of The Jossey-Bass Higher and Adult Education Series and is published quarterly by Wiley Subscription Services, Inc., A Wiley Company, at Jossey-Bass, One Montgomery Street, Suite 1200, San Francisco, CA 94104-4594. Periodicals Postage Paid at San Francisco, California, and at additional mailing offices. POSTMASTER: Send address changes to New Directions for Student Services, Jossey-Bass, One Montgomery Street, Suite 1200, San Francisco, CA 94104-4594.

New Directions for Student Services is indexed in CIJE: Current Index to Journals in Education (ERIC), Contents Pages in Education (T&F), Current Abstracts (EBSCO), Education Index/Abstracts (H.W. Wilson), Educational Research Abstracts Online (T&F), ERIC Database (Education Resources Information Center), and Higher Education Abstracts (Claremont Graduate University).

Microfilm copies of issues and articles are available in 16mm and 35mm, as well as microfiche in 105mm, through University Microfilms Inc., 300 North Zeeb Road, Ann Arbor, Michigan 48106-1346.

SUBSCRIPTIONS cost $89.00 for individuals and $275.00 for institutions, agencies, and libraries in the United States.

EDITORIAL CORRESPONDENCE should be sent to the Editor-in-Chief, Elizabeth J. Whitt, N473 Lindquist Center, The University of Iowa, Iowa City, IA 52242.

www.josseybass.com

CONTENTS

EDITORS' NOTES

Most days, the news typically reports on events reflecting some kind of a moral crossroads. Some of these events involve institutional issues, such as the SAT cheating scandal attributed to administrators and teachers in the Atlanta public school system. Others are on an individual level. For example, former Rutgers student Dharun Ravi was convicted of using a webcam to broadcast roommate Tyler Clementi's sexual encounter with another man. Tyler committed suicide shortly after the broadcast. These are two of many examples of why student affairs professionals must consider purposeful approaches to promoting moral growth and development to prepare students to face difficult choices in the future.

The call for higher education to include moral development as a learning outcome is not new. More than 40 years ago, Brown and Canon (1978) pointed to the need for moral education in postsecondary settings to tend to the "void created by the abandonment of *in loco parentis* models" (p. 426). They called on student affairs professionals to practice caring confrontation rather than wait for students to pay a financial fine levied on them for their bad behavior.

No doubt that college students face complicated moral and ethical situations on a daily basis. This volume provides a framework for facilitating the moral development of college students through various campus initiatives. The authors briefly describe the theoretical frameworks that are useful for working with students' moral and ethical development and then identify practices outside the classroom appropriate for student affairs educators.

We have five starting assumptions for this volume:

1. Moral growth and change is a developmental task that occurs during young adulthood.
2. Moral development is a goal that is increasingly evidenced in mission statements of higher educational institutions yet rarely is assessed as part of measurable learning outcomes.
3. The word "moral" comes with baggage that is culturally and religiously grounded. The higher education community may have shied away from using it as a specific goal and instead has used such terms as "civic engagement," "campus involvement," "service-learning," or "character education." However, we see these terms as potential *means* to the moral end.
4. There is a cultural context to what is known about moral development. There may also be a political or ideological context.
5. Moral growth requires the context of a relationship.

NEW DIRECTIONS FOR STUDENT SERVICES, no. 139, Fall 2012 © Wiley Periodicals, Inc.
Published online in Wiley Online Library (wileyonlinelibrary.com) • DOI: 10.1002/ss.20017

In Chapter One, we describe moral development in the context of higher education, explore how values and assumptions create a frame for moral development, and describe the relationship between cognitive development and moral development. We differentiate between moral reasoning (cognitions) and moral action (character), and explore the provocative nature of learning experiences that are vital to the moral growth and development of college students. Further, we look at three approaches to understanding moral development: those of Lawrence Kohlberg, Carol Gilligan (and the expansions on her work by Nel Noddings), and James Rest.

In Chapter Two, Liddell explores three dimensions in moral development: (1) morality as an individual construct, (2) facilitated by powerful relationships, (3) in the context of the organization. The teachable moment is usually one that is centered in conflict for the learner: dissonance about an issue or discomfort around a choice. The author explores the importance of others in moral development: peers, parents, faculty, and teammates. Finally, for the institution, there should be consistency between espoused and lived values.

Service-learning has become a popular activity on campus to intentionally create opportunities for students to experience activities designed to take them out of their comfort zone with the support necessary to process the events. In Chapter Three, Scott differentiates service-learning and volunteerism, and examines the role of student affairs in each. He explores how service-learning can facilitate growth and cultivate relationships that lead to moral development. In Chapter Four, Boyd and Brackmann expand on the concept of the nature of civic engagement and personal and social responsibility as conditions for increasing moral development. The chapter provides a rationale and process for how to encourage students to examine, develop, and personalize their integrity, excellence, and ethical and moral reasoning capabilities, contribution to the larger community (that is, civic engagement), and ability to take seriously the perspective of others.

Chapter Five explores the co-curricular domains of learning and includes a discussion of several issues: self-governance, restorative justice on campus, the role of forgiveness in victim healing, and uses of a social justice lens. Lancaster also explores how such alternatives can easily satisfy the legal and ethical need for good practices in student conduct.

Stewart discusses the relationship between moral growth and teaching about diversity, multiculturalism, and social justice on the college campus in Chapter Six. She describes effective and ineffective initiatives in this area, including how we can design educational opportunities that honor individual developmental differences and how can we move students toward social justice action.

Chapter Seven, by Dunn and Hart-Steffes, explores the concept of sustainability by demonstrating how we can teach students to understand sustainability as an act of social justice and moral action. Model programs from across the country are highlighted to provide guidance for student affairs professionals to increase moral development though attention given to the environment.

Healy, Lancaster, Liddell, and Stewart charge professionals working with students to assume the role of moral exemplar, to be someone worth emulating, to be reflective and intentional in their relationships with students. Of particular note in Chapter Eight is the role of the professional in facilitating difficult dialogue and understanding the importance of aspirational ethical practice.

The final chapter in this volume provides the reader a description of the various assessment approaches, instruments available for the measurement of moral development, and their utility to the scholar-practitioner. Cooper, Liddell, Davis, and Pasquesi examine several measures of moral development as well as the issues associated with qualitative inquiry and moral development. The chapter examines measurement on the individual, group, and organizational level as well as the challenge of researching versus assessing moral outcomes.

Rest's Four Component Model of moral functioning (1986)—moral sensitivity, moral judgment, moral motivation, and moral action—is used as the framework for this text. The volume explores both macro and micro processes that can be employed by student affairs professionals to enhance moral development of students.

References

Brown, R., and Canon, H. "Intentional Moral Development as an Objective of Higher Education." *Journal of College Student Personnel*, 1978, 19(5), 426–429.
Rest, J. *Moral Development: Advances in Research and Theory.* New York: Praeger, 1986.

DEBORA L. LIDDELL *is an associate professor and program coordinator of the Higher Education and Student Affairs Graduate Program at the University of Iowa.*

DIANE L. COOPER *is a professor of college student affairs administration at the University of Georgia.*

1

Why does moral development matter now? What resources are available for campus professionals committed to facilitating moral growth in college?

Moral Development in Higher Education

Debora L. Liddell, Diane L. Cooper

Student affairs, from its formation as a profession, has always included some attention to the development of the whole student, including moral and religious values (American Council on Education, 1937). In the 1960s and 1970s, higher education put less emphasis on these areas in part due to the outcomes of legal cases that gave students more rights and freedoms within the academy. However, recent events and public debate have renewed the focus of higher education toward a consideration of moral development as an anticipated outcome of college attendance. Colby (2002) noted:

> We see a groundswell of interest in higher education's capacity to contribute to stronger communities, a more responsive democratic system, and more engaged citizens. Critics from outside and within the academy are joining a chorus of calls to revitalize the public purposes of higher education, including educating for students' moral and civic development, as well as technical and more narrowly intellectual learning [p. 1].

As we examine the expansion of the field of student affairs and how professionals work with students, we can clearly see the evolution of our approach to students' moral development. Early in our history, we operated out of a student services framework where students were offered programs or provided offices that provided moral or ethical support in a manner accepted as normative for the time. With the shift from service to student development, professionals began creating opportunities to challenge and support students as they mature. Recently our focus has been on student learning, where we help students author their own story, by not only providing opportunities for growth but also by helping students make meaning of their experiences. College life both inside and outside the classroom is

NEW DIRECTIONS FOR STUDENT SERVICES, no. 139, Fall 2012 © Wiley Periodicals, Inc.
Published online in Wiley Online Library (wileyonlinelibrary.com) • DOI: 10.1002/ss.20018

ripe with powerful learning opportunities, yet we still must ensure that experiences are purposefully designed to promote this type of learning. In fact, Whiteley (2002) noted that "one of the fundamental obligations of the modern college and university is to influence intentionally the moral thinking and action of the next generation of society's leaders and citizens" (p. 5).

Chickering (2010) refers to higher education as the most compelling institutional source for upholding our democracy, although he warns that we have fallen far short of creating college graduates "who can function at the levels of cognitive, moral, intellectual, and ethical development that our complex national and global problems require" (p. 3).

Over the past decade, academic units on most campuses have explored ways to include service-learning as part of classroom learning outcomes. Other programs reflect an increased emphasis on citizenship or personal and social responsibility. At their core, all of these programs and activities may seek to facilitate moral development. Swaner (2004) concluded: "[T]here is ample evidence that cognitive aspects of personal and social responsibility—namely moral reasoning—continue to develop during the college years. This evidence would suggest that educating for personal and social responsibility is indeed a legitimate consideration for higher education" (p. 44).

The Moral Crisis in Higher Education

Activism related to moral issues is not new on college campuses. Student protests against sweatshop production of collegiate wear in the 1990s brought about fair trade policies on campuses across the United States. And students protesting colleges' and universities' financial investments in South Africa in the 1980s increased pressure to end the apartheid regime there. The crisis of character in American society is certainly a pressing issue, as evidenced by recent headlines.

For instance, the Occupy Wall Street protests during the summer of 2011 called attention to widespread social and economic problems in the nation. The Occupy movement expanded to other communities and campuses that fall, and campus response to the protestors varied greatly. For instance, at the University of California at Davis, demands for Chancellor Linda Katehi's resignation increased over her failure to prevent what some have called a shameful attack on the First Amendment (Blumenstyk, 2011). It was on this campus, following weeks of Occupy protests, that peaceful protestors endured the sustained assault by campus police of pepper spray in their faces and mouths. The widely viewed video showed two campus police officers patrolling a seated row of a few dozen students, spraying their faces at close range. The police officers in question were placed on paid leave, raising questions about the role played by Katehi, who reportedly called out the police in riot gear to confront the peaceful protestors. By

NEW DIRECTIONS FOR STUDENT SERVICES • DOI: 10.1002/ss

pitting campus police against its students, the UC-Davis administration abdicated its responsibility to engage students in serious and thoughtful dialogue about social injustice and change agency.

At the time this volume goes to press, Penn State University is still reeling from the conviction of former longtime assistant football coach Jerry Sandusky for the sexual abuse of several young boys. At issue is not only what Coach Sandusky is reported to have committed but also the lack of response on the part of the then head coach, Joe Paterno; a graduate assistant employed by the football program; several senior administrators; and the local district attorneys—all of whom admit being informed of at least one incident of abuse. At the date of this writing, the situation has ended the careers of Penn State's president, the athletic director, and the head football coach.

Finally, hazing, long a concern in collegiate organizations and most often associated with Greek organizations, garnered the headlines recently with the death of a band member at Florida A&M University. Robert Champion, a university drum major, had hazing-related injuries that resulted in his death, which was ruled a homicide. As CNN's Roland Martin (2011) notes, "Here was a young man who went off to college, planning to earn a college degree while leading one of the nation's most colorful and exciting bands, only to be returned home to his parents in Georgia in a coffin" (p. 1). The university president and the band's director (who has been put on temporary leave) have been criticized for being aware of the tradition and culture of hazing with the band and not appropriately responding. Yet students seem to be siding with these two leaders against their critics, including Florida governor Rick Scott. At the time of this writing, 13 people had been charged with criminal hazing—11 of those were felonious charges.

What these incidents have in common is that they call into question the moral credibility of higher education leadership, particularly at a time when the public is alienated by other American institutions—banks, corporations, media, and government. They also create powerful teachable moments on college campuses—opportunities we will explore in this volume.

Higher Education Initiatives on Moral Development

It could be argued that the recent attention to morally loaded events on college campuses has intensified by the corporate and political scandals of the past twenty years. We are left to wonder how we are preparing future leaders and active citizens. Although the stakes are high, there are a growing number of provocative initiatives designed to cultivate moral and ethical development in college students. Some of these initiatives are described in this chapter.

The Association of American Colleges and Universities (AACU) has supported a number of institutes, publications, and research activities exploring how higher education institutions can foster personal and social responsibility on campus (Hersh and Schneider, 2005). The result of this work is AACU's five Core Commitments, which are at the heart of developmental goals for students:

1. Striving for excellence: developing a strong work ethic and consciously doing one's very best in all aspects of college
2. Cultivating personal and academic integrity: recognizing and acting on a sense of honor, ranging from honesty in relationships to principled engagement with a formal academic honor code
3. Contributing to a larger community: recognizing and acting on one's responsibility to the educational community and the wider society, locally, nationally, and globally
4. Taking seriously the perspectives of others: recognizing and acting on the obligation to inform one's own judgment; engaging diverse and competing perspectives as a resource for learning, citizenship, and work
5. Developing moral competence in thought and deed: developing ethical and moral reasoning in ways that incorporate the other four responsibilities; using such reasoning in learning and in life [Dey, E. L. and Associates, 2010, p. 1].

The International Center for Academic Integrity (ICAI; 2011), housed at Clemson University (www.academicintegrity.org), is an international initiative to cultivate values related to academic work. The ICAI Web site includes information about academic integrity assessment, links to a searchable database of related research, as well as several downloadable papers that could ignite campuswide discussions on honesty, integrity, and moral development of students.

Sports and moral development go hand in hand in American society. The Center for Ethics at the University of Idaho (www.educ.uidaho.edu/center_for_ethics) provides outreach and conducts research on moral education and athletic competition. The staff is particularly involved in working with collegiate sport teams.

Also of note is the Templeton Foundation, which has funded major research and demonstration projects that explore character development (www.templeton.org).

The increased emphasis on aspects of moral development is also evident in the growth of the Jon C. Dalton Institute on College Student Values as well as the creation of the *Journal of College and Character*. Begun in 1991, the Dalton Institute provides a forum for both faculty and student affairs educators seeking more effective ways to enhance ethical development of college students (http://studentvalues.fsu.edu). The journal's focus is on the development of character in college, and the influences of colleges and universities on moral and civic learning. The journal has been published since 2000 (http://journals.naspa.org/jcc).

On a broader scope, the Association for Moral Education (AME) is an interdisciplinary organization that has been in existence for almost forty years (www.amenetwork.org). The focus of AME's work is also on moral education and development beyond just higher education, including the creation of new theories and models and the dissemination of related research.

All of these initiatives have been helpful in supporting our work with students in their search for purpose and meaning, but there is urgency about this work now. We in higher education are now situated to have discussions and design purposeful interventions, have difficult conversations with students as they make meaning of their lives, and modify our programs and services (with special attention to social justice and pluralism) to consider the moral implications of our work. All of this helps us confront a moral anemia that has become commonplace in our country. The chapters that follow provide a platform for considering where we can take our practice (for example, student conduct, sustainability, civic engagement, service-learning) to facilitate the moral growth of our students. What follows is a brief review of the theoretical frameworks that provide the foundation for this volume.

Theoretical Frameworks

Most of what we know and teach about moral development is grounded in the work of cognitive-structural theorists, such as Jean Piaget and William Perry. Cognitive-structural theories are more concerned with *how* learning happens, not *what* is learned. Cognitive-structural theories assume that development happens in stage sequencing that is invariant, hierarchical, and qualitatively unique from other stages (as opposed to additive). Using cognitive structures help us to organize and adapt to our environments. Additionally, understanding moral growth from a cognitive-structural developmental framework leads us to expect that learners (in our case, college students) are using cognitive structures to make meaning and reason through problems as they become more intellectually complex and competent (McEwen, 2003). In this section we briefly describe the most frequently cited theory of moral development—Lawrence Kohlberg's—and the subsequent theories of Carol Gilligan, Nel Noddings, and James Rest.

Lawrence Kohlberg's Theory of Moral Reasoning. Grounded in a cognitive-structural approach (and the assumption that reasoning precedes action), Kohlberg's core concepts state that the moral learner moves through three levels and six stages of development. The first, the Pre-Conventional Level, is most evident in children. With its focus on self-centered morality, the learner makes judgments based on the direct consequences to themselves. Actions, therefore, are motivated by a fear of punishment or by self-interest ("What's in it for me?"). This first level of moral reasoning is characterized by a lack of concern for the effect on others. More typically seen in adolescents and adults, the Conventional Level of moral reasoning is characterized by conforming to the larger society's "conventional" expectations. In other words, I am expected to be a "good person," so my actions are motivated by that goal. In this level, the learner rarely questions the validity of society's rules, laws, and norms about what is right and wrong. Finally, the Post-Conventional Level reflects a "principled" realization that individuals are separate from the greater society and that it is possible to disobey rules and laws that conflict with our principles. Kohlbergian educators believe in the universality of certain principles, such as justice.

Carol Gilligan's Ethic of Care. Inspired by psychologists Erik Erikson and her Harvard colleague Lawrence Kohlberg, Carol Gilligan took issue with what she called Kohlberg's adherence to "justice" as a universal moral mandate. Of Kohlberg, she said: "Psychology was a moral science and it was impossible to talk about development without addressing in one way or another the questions of how to live and what to do" (Gilligan, 1997, p. 2).

These questions—about how to live and what to do—gripped Gilligan in 1970 as she taught a section of Kohlberg's undergraduate course on moral and political choice. The discussion turned to the contemporary events at Kent State University and the killing by the U.S. National Guard of four college students who protested the escalation of the Vietnam War. Gilligan later recounted that:

> In my section, the young men refused to talk about the draft, aware that there was no room in Larry's theory for them to talk about what they were feeling without sounding morally undeveloped, like women, in their concern about relationships and other people's feelings. Uneasy about taking a stand in public that was at odds with what they were feeling in private, finding no room for uncertainty and indecision, they chose silence over hypocrisy [Gilligan, 1997, p. 3].

For these young men, this was a real and personal dilemma—not a hypothetical dilemma posed by Kohlberg—and the consequences of acting on their aversion for the war affected not only the men but also their loved ones. This experience created the stage on which Gilligan would develop her own research questions about moral choice: exploring the possibility that there is a difference between what one *wants* to do and what one feels they *should* do.

She went on to develop a theory around a morality of care—rooted in a compass toward connectedness and relational interactions with others (Gilligan, 1982). Her theory centered on the saliency of relationships and connectedness and the interpersonal ideas (as opposed to societal ideas) about what it means to be a good person (for example, what do others want me to do?). Central to this theory are the early childhood experiences that allow children to feel attached to those who care for them. This morality of care has three levels: survival, goodness, and truth, with transitions between the three levels that allow the reparation of relationships. There is a growing consensus among many researchers that care, like justice, is a universal principle that deserves study. More about Kohlberg's and Gilligan's research on moral development, particularly the measurement of their theories, is explored in Chapter Nine.

Nel Noddings's Caring Ethics. Nel Noddings's work frequently is associated with Gilligan's, as both were interested in exploring the ethics of care as the rational foundation for moral decision making. Originally framed as a feminine approach to ethics, Noddings's work stemmed from her assumption that care is a primal need and a viable way to be guided in our attitudes, decisions, and choices. She posited that care is basic in all of human life, that care is a moral attitude that can lead us to action, and that care should be cultivated in schools (Noddings, 1984, 1992). Further, Noddings suggested that home should be the primary educator of young people and the place where care is first developed.

Noddings's model of development from the care perspective has four factors: (1) social modeling by others, (2) dialogue about caring, (3) practicing and developing good habits of caring and reflection, and (4) affirmation that requires trust in others (1992).

Moral Development or Moral Maturity

Both James Rest and Kieran Mathieson expanded on Kolhberg's previous work to look beyond the constructs of reasoning and judgment. Mathieson (2003) identified seven factors of moral maturity:

1. Moral agency and a sense of the self as moral being
2. The ability to harness cognitive ability to make decisions
3. The ability to harness emotional resources and sensitivity toward others
4. Using social skill to persuade others
5. Identifying and using higher-order principles as guidance for our choices
6. Valuing and respecting others
7. Developing a sense of one's life purpose

All of these elements can contribute to a moral curriculum on our college campuses.

James Rest's Components of Moral Maturity. In an approach referred to as neo-Kohlbergian, James Rest and his colleagues (Rest, Narvaez, Bebeau, and Thoma, 1999) asserted that moral reasoning was only one of four necessary components of moral maturity: moral sensitivity (awareness), moral judgment (reasoning), moral motivation, and moral action. Bolstered by research using the Defining Issues Test (DIT), Rest and his colleagues from the Center for the Study of Ethical Development refined the DIT (and revised it to address shortcomings in the DIT-2). The center began at the University of Minnesota in the 1970s and was moved to the University of Alabama following Rest's death in 1999 (Thoma, 2002). The center's focus is on empirical research and publication. The DIT-2 is discussed more thoroughly in Chapter Nine. Rest's work provides a useful map in our work with students. As such, we have used it to help frame this volume.

Moral Sensitivity. The first component in Rest's framework for moral maturity is moral sensitivity, which refers to one's alertness to the need for a particular action and an ability to quickly interpret a situation as having more than one course of action. Moral sensitivity requires a near-instinctual response to situations. It requires one to respond to cues in the environment, either with one's gut or to think through who and what would be affected by various possible actions, including the potential feelings of others. Therefore, a primary cognitive-affective aspect of this sensitivity is to *feel something* for other people—whether empathy, fear, or disgust.

Much has been written on the importance of empathy and sensitivity to others as a prerequisite condition for moral development. This concept is explored in more detail in Chapter Two.

Moral Judgment. The second component of moral maturity identified by Rest is that of moral judgment or reasoning. This process involves more of the cognitive dimensions of morality and is helpful to understanding, though it is short on emotion and affect. Moral judgment involves deciding which course of action is right, just, or fair in a particular situation—a process that requires weighing choices and possible consequences of each to determine which course of action is the morally best one. Only then can one commit to an action based on an understanding of the principles involved.

Moral Motivation. A third component necessary for moral maturity is moral motivation, involving the commitment that one makes toward the moral course of action. This commitment typically is rooted in strong emotion. It's the gut-check aspect of moral action—the compass, the conscience, and the will to put aside personal interests in favor of moral values. This moral motivation calls to mind the development of personal credo that serves as a moral anchor when facing choices, when one prioritizes moral values over personal values. If a business owner chooses to distribute profits to factory workers at the expense of deep personal gain, we conclude this owner is motivated to put moral values ahead of personal ones—as characterized as a conflict in values. Because we are driven to maintain a consistent self-image, our beliefs about ourselves are in play here. This idea is explored in more detail in Chapter Two.

NEW DIRECTIONS FOR STUDENT SERVICES • DOI: 10.1002/ss

Moral Action. Moral action is the culminating and definitive component, wherein one's sensitivity, judgment, and motivation integrate into execution. Sometimes referred to as moral character, this component entails having the courage and integrity to act on that personal credo or the determined moral action (Narvaez and Rest, 1995). This is life as we know it: moving beyond hypothetical dilemmas about whether Heinz should steal the drug, or who in our community should be allowed to enter the lifeboat. Moral action requires resolving real-life conflicts that may be high stakes for the learner.

How do these four components work together? Narvaez and Rest (1995) maintain that moral action requires self-confidence, perseverance, and steadfastness toward the final goal, and a belief in one's success in the task. It is the component frequently referred to as "character."

Moral Development or Character Education?

So, why not just teach the traits associated with character? The character education movement in K–12 typically is regarded as one expedient way to direct younger students toward a common moral goal. The appropriateness of teaching toward specified pillars or core values, however, has been criticized by some who think this kind of educational directive undermines independent critical thought. There may, however, be inherent value in engaging students in explicit teaching and direction about institutional values that benefit individuals *and* community, such as freedom, autonomy, respect for others, justice, or truth.

Should not character education transcend the personal development of individuals and move students toward public action to benefit others? If it does, then our task is clear. We should not only help students negotiate their interpersonal relations as they move through their worlds but also help them with the cognitive components to negotiate those complex worlds. For example, when we ask students to work at a Free Lunch Program that serves meals for low-income and homeless families, we should arm them with the knowledge and skills to talk to the clients there, to investigate the causes of hunger and poverty, and to discuss the socioeconomic and political means of meeting these challenges. Doing the right thing is more than about showing up and serving lunch. Narvaez and Rest (1995) wrote: "It would be a mistake to portray the whole of morality as simply empathy, or simply concepts of justice, or merely genetic predisposition to be altruistic, or solely mimicking a model. . . . If moral behavior is the end goal of moral education, then moral education ought to be addressing all four components" (p. 398).

We concur wholeheartedly with this sentiment and therefore assume the four-component approach to morality as a framework throughout this volume.

NEW DIRECTIONS FOR STUDENT SERVICES • DOI: 10.1002/ss

Definitions Used in This Volume

The term "moral development" often is used as an interchangeable term for "ethical development," yet these are somewhat distinct constructs. In this sourcebook, we are focusing on moral development, which is an aspect of cognitive development. As a person is able to make sense of the world in more complex ways, the ability to weigh moral actions also moves to more sophisticated decision-making approaches.

"Ethics" refers to a set of moral principles used by an individual or group that provides a framework for behavior. For instance, professional associations expect ethical behavior of their members and set the parameters for that behavior in their ethical guidelines. These guidelines are determined by the mores of the field and the gatekeeping functions related to the public. For example, the ethical expectations of a counseling psychologist will be markedly different from those of a student affairs professional because of the professional and in some cases legally defined nature of the relationship between the clinician and the client.

The concept of "character" refers to the "habits of mind, heart, and conduct that help students know and do what is ethical" (Dalton, 1999, p. 47). Because good moral health includes cognitions, values, emotions, and the will to act, we think of morality holistically—it simply must be addressed in a multifaceted way that includes support for students on all domains.

Summary

In this chapter, we have laid out the basic foundational concepts and assumptions that will guide the reader through the chapters to come as the authors explore *how* moral growth can be facilitated through various initiatives on the college campus.

References

American Council on Education. "The Student Personnel Point of View," 1937, *1*(3). Retrieved December 10, 2011, from http://www.myacpa.org/pub/documents/1937.pdf

Blumenstyk, G. "UC-Davis Chancellor Apologizes as Outrage Builds Over Pepper-Spray Use on Peaceful Protestors." *Chronicle of Higher Education*, November 22, 2011. Retrieved December 30, 2011, from http://chronicle.com.proxy.lib.uiowa.edu/article/UC-Davis-Chancellor-Apologizes/129870/.

Chickering, A. W. "A Retrospective on Higher Education's Commitment to Moral and Civic Education." *Journal of College and Character*, 2010, *11*(3), 1–6.

Colby, A. "Whose Values Anyway?" *Journal of College and Character*, 2002, *3*(5), 1–16.

Dalton, J. C. "Helping Students Develop Coherent Values and Ethical Standards." In G. S. Blimling and E. J. Whitt (eds.), *Principles of Good Practice in Student Affairs*. San Francisco: John Wiley & Sons, 1999.

Dey, E. L., and Associates. *Engaging diverse viewpoints: What Is the Campus Climate for Perspective-Taking?* Washington, D.C.: Association of American Colleges and Universities, 2010. Retrieved June 21, 2012, from http://www.aacu.org/core_commitments/documents/Engaging_Diverse_Viewpoints.pdf.

Gilligan, C. *In a Different Voice: Psychological Theory and Women's Development.* Cambridge, Mass.: Harvard University Press, 1982.

Gilligan, C. "Remembering Larry." Speech at the Association for Moral Education, Atlanta, Ga., November 1997. Retrieved December 29, 2011, from http://www.des.emory.edu/mfp/302/302gillkohl.PDF.

Hersh, R. H., and Schneider, C. G. "Fostering Personal and Social Responsibility on College and University Campuses." *Liberal Education,* 2005, *91,* 6–13.

Martin, R. "Only Students Can Truly End Hazing." CNN, 2011. Retrieved December 28, 2011, from http://articles.cnn.com/2011–12–16/opinion/opinion_roland-martin-hazing_1_hazing-incident-end-hazing-famu-students?_s = PM:OPINION.

Mathieson, K. "Elements of Moral Maturity." *Journal of College and Character,* 2003, *4*(5), retrieved December 20, 2011, from http://journals.naspa.org/jcc.

McEwen, M. K. "The Nature and Uses of Theory." In S. K. Komives, D. B. Woodard Jr., and Associates (eds.), *Student Services: A Handbook for the Profession* (4th ed.). San Francisco: Jossey-Bass, 2003.

Narvaez, D., & Rest, J. "The Four Components of Acting Morally." In W. M. Kurtines and J. L. Gewirtz (eds.), *Moral Development: An Introduction.* Boston: Allyn & Bacon, 1995.

Noddings, N. *Caring: A Feminine Approach to Ethics and Moral Education.* Berkeley: University of California Press, 1984.

Noddings, N. *The Challenge to Care in Schools: An Alternative Approach to Education.* New York: Teachers College Press, 1992.

Rest, J., Narvaez, D., Bebeau, M., and Thoma, S. *Postconventional Moral Thinking: A Neo-Kohlbergian Approach.* Mahwah, N.J.: Lawrence Erlbaum, 1999.

Swaner, L. E. "Educating for Personal and Social Responsibility: A Planning Project of the Association of American Colleges and Universities." 2004. Retrieved June 21, 2012, from http://www.aacu.org/core_commitments/documents/review_of_lit.pdf

Thoma, S. J. "An Overview of the Minnesota Approach to Research in Moral Development." *Journal of Moral Education,* 2002, *31*(3), 225–245.

Whiteley, J. M. "Exploring Moral Action in the Context of the Dilemmas of Young Adulthood." *Analytic Teaching,* 2002, *20*(1), 4–25.

DEBORA L. LIDDELL *is an associate professor and program coordinator of the Higher Education and Student Affairs Graduate Program at the University of Iowa.*

DIANE L. COOPER *is a professor of college student affairs administration at the University of Georgia.*

NEW DIRECTIONS FOR STUDENT SERVICES • DOI: 10.1002/ss

2

We have an opportunity and an obligation to challenge and support students as they wrestle with moral choices.

Identifying and Working Through Teachable Moments

Debora L. Liddell

This chapter explores three dimensions in moral development: (1) morality as an individual construct, (2) facilitated by powerful relationships, (3) in the context of the organization. Our goal in this chapter is to orient the educator to the mind of the learner and suggest strategies and approaches that facilitate learning.

Assumptions We Make About Learners and Learning

Student affairs educators should explore their assumptions about how learning occurs—especially outside the classroom. Our assumptions about learning are grounded in humanistic and psychological theories usually attributed to Carl Rogers, Albert Bandura, David Kolb, and Carol Tavris.

1. Significant learning takes place when the subject is seen as being relevant and meaningful to the learner (Rogers, 1969).
2. Learning can best occur when the learner does not feel threatened. Typical responses to a threat—that is, flight or fight—are often manifest in the learner's defensiveness, resistance, or denial (Rogers, 1969).
3. Learning is maximized when learners participate actively, when learners act as agents of their own growth and development, and when conclusions are drawn by the learners—as opposed to an authority figure (Piaget, 1977; Kolb, 1984).
4. When self-evaluation is more valued than the evaluation of authority figures, independence, creativity, and self-reliance are likely to result (Rogers, 1969).

New Directions for Student Services, no. 139, Fall 2012 © Wiley Periodicals, Inc.
Published online in Wiley Online Library (wileyonlinelibrary.com) • DOI: 10.1002/ss.20019

5. People have a need to maintain a congruent self (Rogers, 1961). They will work to reduce dissonance by changing either their behaviors or their beliefs, a condition that can motivate people to craft purposeful goals.
6. Beliefs about ourselves are important mediators of motivation.

The central premise here is that developmental momentum shifts from an allegiance to authority (dualism) to more intellectual individuation and self-reliance. And while this individuation is necessary, it is not sufficient for moral growth. We require interaction with others for developmental movement, a condition explored in this chapter.

A Mile in Their Shoes: Understanding the Individual Learner

In order to facilitate moral growth, it is important to identify and understand the teachable moment. Students come to college with a distinctive set of conditions, experiences, values, and needs that must be understood by the educators who seek to work with them. Much of moral learning is centered in cognitive conflict for the learner—a notion explored originally by Piaget and later by Kohlberg and others. A student comes face to face with an experience that does not fit his or her cognitive schema. This creates cognitive conflict, or dissonance—a state of unpleasant tension between current beliefs and new, conflicting information—when two inconsistent ideas, values, or attitudes come together. Used originally by Leon Festinger (1957) and explored more recently by Carol Tavris and Elliott Aronson (2007), the phrase "cognitive dissonance" is used to explain one's motivation in the face of conflicting ideas. The tension that comes from the inconsistency of competing beliefs and desires creates a drive or motivation to change either our behaviors or our beliefs, as most of us do not have a long-term ability to hold two conflicting ideas at the same time. We are motivated in this moment of dissonance to do what we need to in order to reduce the feeling of cognitive conflict.

Piaget (1977) and Kohlberg (1981) referred to this as disequilibrium. Chickering and Reisser (1993) viewed these patterns of differentiation and integration as necessary for development. The term "differentiation" refers to this notion of challenge to one's belief system or cognitive structures. This period of unbalance is settled through the process of integration—integrating conflicting values into a more complex way of viewing the world.

A simple example of this may be that Frederick is a vegetarian—a choice he made for humanitarian reasons. A friend points out, however, that while Frederick may not eat meat, he chooses to carry a case made of leather. Are not these conflicting choices? As the theory goes, Frederick cannot likely hold both of these beliefs at the same time—either the behavior will change or the beliefs will change. This may lead Frederick to justify his decision to carry a leather case by cultivating support arguments, such as "Animals are not slaughtered for leather-made goods—they are a by-product of the meat industry." This new belief serves to justify his choices and may help settle his cognitive conflict.

Leaning into Discomfort and Dissonance. How might we use these concepts to facilitate learning? Much of the motivation to learn is grounded in our expectations of ourselves and our deep need to maintain a consistent and congruent self-image. This need for our beliefs, values, cognitions, and behaviors to be congruent motivates us. I argue that while emotions are secondary to cognitions, they also can be motivating factors for learning.

For instance, anger or frustration can compromise the motivation to work through differences and cognitive conflict, especially if competition may undergird that conflict. Consider the case of Maria, a graduate student who had received some sharp criticism from her assistantship supervisor. Maria was told that her inflexibility had negatively affected her coworkers and made it difficult to build a cooperative work team. The initial sting from this criticism created such a defensive wall that it was difficult for Maria to stay open to what could have been construed as important, constructive feedback from a supervisor. She reported she had never heard feedback like this before and that it was completely contradictory to how she viewed herself—as a collaborative, capable professional in training. Perhaps the supervisor just did not like her, she said. How else could Maria reconcile this feedback with what she knew to be true about herself?

I shared with Maria my own reactions to situations when I had heard something that didn't square with my deeply held beliefs about myself. I told her that a generous spirit and a bit of patience helped me sit through what felt like a rather personal assault. Most of us dislike conflict, and therefore, we are more likely to look the other way and not deal directly with problematic behavior. A supervisor or mentor who believes in a mentee's potential, however, sees it differently. A supervisor who is invested in you, I told Maria, believes that you will grow if you can address this shortcoming. I encouraged her to acknowledge and name her discomfort (whether it is pain or embarrassment) and to ask her supervisor for specific examples of behavior that demonstrate the criticism. These examples could help Maria identify what others may see as problematic. I asked her to consider if she might lean into this discomfort as a moment of learning and as an investment in this relationship. Maria and her supervisor individually reported to me later that the conversation was productive, that they had a new understanding of each other's frustrations, but they also came to appreciate the deep investment each had in the relationship.

Reflection and Learning. Encouraging students to sit with their discomfort and ask themselves "What can I learn from this?" will strengthen their resistance to fight or flee the conflict. The art of "sitting with" our cognitive discomfort requires more than just being still. In order to make meaning from an experience, reflection on that experience is required. Dewey (1933/1910) referred to reflection as a rigorous and intentional way of thinking—more than a stream of consciousness or a passive "chewing on." Reflection can create important meaning-making opportunities—to allow one to move from a discrete experience to a deeper comprehension. Reflection is an "active, persistent, and careful consideration of any belief or supposed form of knowledge in the light of the grounds that support it" (p. 9). As an interactionist, Dewey believed that the first step in learning is an experience—an interaction between the learner and the environment. The learning from that experience cycles through this process: (1) interpret the data that come from the experience, (2) analyze that interpretation, (3) name the questions and problems that arise from the analysis, (4) explore and generate explanations about these questions and problems, and (5) experiment and act on the explanations.

The most powerful and lasting learning emanates from the experience that causes us discomfort. It is the drive to settle the unsettled that allows the learner to sit, to think through, and to ponder the various questions that allow the exploration of different perspectives in an effort to gain balance. Reflection "gives an individual an increased power of control" (Dewey, 1933/1910, p. 21), but it requires several components, including (1) perplexity: reacting to ideas and suggestions when dealing with conflicting beliefs, (2) elaboration: referencing past experiences that may be similar in nature, (3) hypothesis building and vetting, and (4) action. Dewey went on to explain that experimentation—the action that follows reflection—allows the learner to move toward a quieting of that former disequilibrium to master and enjoy the resolution earned. It is the fitting together of the new puzzle pieces, the trying on of new knowledge and ways of thinking. This commitment to action brings the reflective cycle full circle.

For a more extensive reading about the reflective learning cycle, readers are referred to the work of David Kolb (1984), who extended Dewey's theory.

Prompting Reflection That Leads to Learning. Several tools designed to foster reflection are helpful to suggest to students with whom we work. The most common and accessible tool may be the written journal. In terms of reflection, journaling can serve several specific purposes. It can create a blank canvas on which to express the data that are generated from an experience. For instance, brainstorming on paper one's reactions to a powerful film can help the learner identify the immediate responses that can be explored further. Question prompts here might include: *What do you see is going on here? How do you react to what you see? Who is involved and what are they doing?*

Naming the problem of the question—locating the center of the problem—is a vital process for moral learning. It requires the learner to line

NEW DIRECTIONS FOR STUDENT SERVICES • DOI: 10.1002/ss

up the data generated to the questions that emanate from a moral or ethical dilemma.

A second purpose for journaling is to provide the further exploration of the analysis of the data (or reactions) generated from the original experience. This analysis can be facilitated by questions such as: *What surprises you and why* (an exploration of assumptions and biases)? *How is this experience similar to past experiences? What perspectives or beliefs might others have about this situation?* Prompts such as these can help a learner work individually through the journaling.

Before a moral or ethical crisis can be resolved, hypothesis building is necessary. This process is facilitated by external resources—talking with others or reading books—to get different and novel perspectives. Dewey and Kolb suggest that this hypothesis building typically is followed by some personal testing of new conclusions. Moral coaches can facilitate conclusions by posing questions such as: *What have I concluded about these experiences? What will I do differently because of it? What will I do the next time I am in this situation?*

Finally, I encourage the process of meta-reflection—the later examination of previous journaling to harvest new conclusions. This "reflecting about reflecting" (Stevens and Cooper, 2009, p. 99) is an opportunity to view a moral problem from 5,000 feet—to see it from a distance with greater clarity and to evaluate the contribution of these reflective practices to deep learning. One classroom example of meta-reflection is an assignment that has students reviewing the journals they previously submitted to find answers to bigger questions about their experience.

The Power of Relationships to Facilitate Learning

The second dimension of moral learning proposed here is that of relationship. Dewey (1933/1910) wrote that just sorting out questions is not sufficient to our complete learning, but being called upon to express our conclusions and new ideas to others can be powerful in cementing our learning. Rodgers (2002) refers to three benefits of sharing reflections with others: affirming the experience and its value to the learner, gaining new perspectives on the experience, and supporting the process of inquiry.

Several years ago I participated in a learning journey to South Africa and Zimbabwe with a team of twelve North Americans who were unknown to me at the time. The purpose of the trip was to explore alternative approaches to leadership and communal approaches to problem solving. The power and intensity of this experience for me was akin to the proverbial sipping from the fire hose. Over the course of the trip, I video-recorded, photographed, journaled, and e-mailed about the various experiences. When I returned home, the only response I could conjure up to the question "How was the trip?" was "Great. Really great." The real learning from this experience was not what had happened in Africa; it was what happened when I had to explain it. It would take the better part of a year of writing, conversing with my fellow travelers, uploading photo narratives to social media, developing a one-hour video to share with my cotravelers, and finally presenting about the trip to colleagues in my college. It was only then—in this communal reflection—that I felt I could lift up the conclusions I had drawn from this powerful experience.

Some communal learning is more potent than others. Dalton (1999) maintains that caring about others is a necessary condition for moral and ethical growth. Without empathizing and connecting with others' points of view, students risk becoming "isolated in their own subjectivity" (p. 51). Indeed, the gift of empathy and prosocial thought are necessary to dialogue, and dialogue is necessary for resolving differences.

Learning from and with Peers. Friendships are powerful things, most especially for young adults. As adolescents leave home, their source of influence shifts from parents to peers. Kuh (1995) refers to peer culture as the "formal and informal groups with whom students identify, affiliate, and seek acceptance and approval over a prolonged period" (p. 564). Kuh, as did many other scholars (for example, Pascarella and Terenzini, 2005), posited that the processes that help form peer culture in college are powerful agents that shape individual and group life on campus. A peer group can influence attitudes, beliefs, and values about everyday moral choices: binge drinking, academic integrity, sexual harassment, or political protests. By understanding and confronting the influences that are antagonistic to learning, educators can raise the bar toward aspirationally ethical standards.

So powerful are peers to learning that Dalton, Crosby, and Mauk (2010) advocate delivering a corollary college curriculum about friendship. It is in the context of friendships that new ideas are piloted, values are challenged, and friends who are important to us are held accountable for their actions.

Learning from and with Mentors. By affirming, transmitting, and reinforcing positive values on campus, higher education leaders can help steer young adults across the moral terrain. For instance, by using the power of social modeling, identifying everyday ethical heroes on campus calls attention to good deeds and thoughtful actions. Using social norming campaigns can also help students understand what the "real norms" are regarding attitudes and behaviors.

Developmental Conversation. In a previous publication, Healy and Liddell (1998) presented a model for "the developmental conversation," rooted in dialogue, informed by empathy, and directed by learning as a goal. That model may be a useful tool for readers in this context and is presented next (please see Exhibit 2.1). It is particularly useful for working with students negotiating a troubling experience.

NEW DIRECTIONS FOR STUDENT SERVICES • DOI: 10.1002/ss

Exhibit 2.1: The Developmental Conversation

Stage of the Conversation	Questions to Explore
Acknowledgment/Construction	What happened? What is the situation? What is at stake?
Perspective taking Points of view	How are others affected? How might others see the situation?
Evaluation	What is there to learn here?
Meaning making	How can that learning be additive to you?
Integration: Resolution, repartition, absolution	How can things be made whole again? What would a good resolution—for all parties— look like?

Source: Healy and Liddell, 1998.

Mentors in the position of working with students in trouble would be well served to keep in mind the goals of learning, restoring justice and relationships, and taking responsibility for actions. This commitment to restorative justice, as opposed to retribution, may facilitate the making whole again of a broken person or relationship.

Moral Learning from Others. In addition to the powerful relationships with peers and mentors, I maintain that others are also important agents of moral learning during the college years. Parents, for instance, can be our best advocate for accountability or learning's worst enemy. This current generation of college students is often characterized as being in close communication with their parents, and their parents are often characterized as being overly invested in their children's success. How might we harvest that connection in a way that supports the mutual goals we and parents have for students—to help them realize their potential as mature, accountable adults capable of independent, moral judgment and action?

Coaches and teammates also may wield their own influence over student athletes. A college sports team is a rich setting to explore the individual obligation to a group. Consider the star quarterback who is arrested for drunk driving and suspended from the team just prior to a bowl game. Encouraging the student to assume personal responsibility toward the team, the school, the fans, and the opposing team may deepen the lesson and model accountability.

Finally, the unique living communities on college campuses (such as residence halls, interest housing, and Greek-letter chapter houses) provide particularly rich opportunities for moral growth. Creating environments that cultivate accountability to one another in healthy ways is a key ingredient to keeping peer influence positive.

New Directions for Student Services • DOI: 10.1002/ss

Moral Development in the Institutional Context

A third component of moral learning is the institution in which we work and live. Do our institutions respond to students in a way that promotes both care and justice and both the needs of the individual and the needs of the community? An institution that puts too much emphasis on justice, rights, and the individual may compromise its ability to create a community of care. Do our institutions facilitate a moral climate that encourages the working through of dissonance when it may be expedient for our institutions to shut down or resolve the conflict? An institution that is overly efficient at its delivery of justice may concede the learning opportunity for its members.

Dalton (1999) maintains that the work of helping students develop ethically while in college requires:

1. Inculcating students toward core values in the institution (most often seen in our student conduct policies and institutional practices).
2. Helping students examine, reflect on, and clarify their values and beliefs.
3. Stimulating a critical evaluation of moral choices.
4. Honoring the affective components of moral sentiment.
5. Involving students in real-life opportunities for moral commitments and action.

These institutional conditions should be coupled with an unwavering consistency between espoused and lived values at the institutional level. Codifying core values through honor codes, compacts, and campus covenants can facilitate their systematic practice.

High-Impact Practices. The National Center for Student Engagement (Kuh, 2008) has challenged higher education to cultivate deeper connections between students' academic experiences and their values and beliefs. These high-impact practices can strengthen student connection. Examples of these practices are described throughout this volume.

Is there a learning laboratory more powerful than the first year of college? Here is a time of coming face to face with differences, a time of doubt, examination, and reflection on the cause of conflict between what one has always held true (values and beliefs) and what one is being introduced to by the institution in which we have placed our trust. This examination requires a high-trust environment (such as a learning community or a first-year seminar) as students reflect on career choice, religious beliefs, sexual activity, gender identity, and drug and alcohol use. The first year of college, with all its disequilibrating experiences, is a particularly rich time for learning.

Challenges to Learning

Our effectiveness as educators requires us to recognize the challenges to learning as students move out of their comfort. We may likely face resistance or retreat if we fail to support students and anticipate the challenges identified next.

Students may be resistant because they hold tight to unexamined values. They hold tight because of the familiarity and comfort associated with these beliefs and values. Normalizing challenge to personally held opinions and values may help the learner clarify their beliefs and anticipate push back about them.

Learners may resist harvesting anything positive from their mistakes if they perceive too much focus on failure. They may fear the punishment that—aside from potential "real" consequences (suspension or a monetary fine)—may involve a loss of face or a feeling of public shame. They may also fail to recognize the separation between the choice and the person ("I screwed up, therefore I am a bad person").

A lack of trust in the other parties involved can create resistance to learning, as can a lack of empathy or ability to take another's perspective.

Students' belonging needs can feed their conformity to a peer group, making students vulnerable to the influence of groupthink. That said, an overemphasis on individuality may block moral growth by retarding a connection and accountability to others.

Other individual stances can also have a chilling effect on our efforts. If students perceive we are dogmatic in our approach, dialogue is discouraged. Allowing language to go unchecked is another harmful stance. We can counter this by being more interested in *understanding others* than being understood. For instance, consider the student accused of calling her gay roommate a derogatory name. Telling her "That's a homophobic thing to do" is quite different from saying "Tell me more about what you mean. I want to understand how you reached your conclusions." Assuming we have nothing to learn from our own students may leave everyone involved in a compromised position.

Finally, an institutional ethos of customer service may make it difficult to be open to learning from mistakes, especially when we view students as customers and we believe that the customer is always right.

Summary

In this chapter I reviewed how morality is an individual construct, facilitated by powerful relationships, in the context of our institutions. By understanding motivation and anticipating resistance and retreat, we can help students lean into their discomfort and learn from their choices, encouraging their aspirations toward goodness, which does not require their perfection. Rather, aspiring to be a good person means that we confront and engage with our imperfections every day.

NEW DIRECTIONS FOR STUDENT SERVICES • DOI: 10.1002/ss

References

Chickering, A.W., and Reisser, L. *Education and Identity* (2 ed.). San Francisco, CA: Jossey-Bass, 1993.

Dalton, J. C. "Helping Students Develop Coherent Values and Ethical Standards." In G. S. Blimling, E. J. Whitt, and Associates (eds.), *Good Practice in Student Affairs: Principles to Foster Student Learning*. San Francisco: Jossey-Bass, 1999.

Dalton, J. C., Crosby, P. C., and Mauk, A. "From Self to Others: Moral Development as the Art of Making and Sustaining Friendships in College." *Journal of College and Character*, 2010, *11*(1), 1–7.

Dewey, J. *How We Think*. Buffalo, N.Y.: Prometheus Books, 1933. (Originally published 1910.)

Festinger, L. *A Theory of Cognitive Dissonance*. Evanston, Ill.: Row and Peterson, 1957.

Healy, M. A., and Liddell, D. L. "The Developmental Conversation: Facilitating Moral and Intellectual Growth in Our Students." In D. Cooper and J. Lancaster (eds.), *Beyond Law and Policy: Reaffirming the Role of Student Affairs*. New Directions for Student Services, no. 82. San Francisco: Jossey-Bass, 1998.

Kohlberg, L. *Essays In Moral Development: The Philosophy of Moral Development, Vol. 1.* New York: Harper & Row, 1981.

Kolb, D. *Experiential Learning: Experience as the Source of Learning and Development*. Englewood Cliffs, N.J.: Prentice-Hall, 1984.

Kuh, G. D. "Cultivating 'High-Stakes' Student Culture Research." *Research in Higher Education*, 1995, *36*, 563–576.

Kuh, G. D. *High-Impact Educational Practices: What They Are, Who Has Access to Them, and Why They Matter*. Washington, D.C.: Association of American Colleges and Universities, 2008.

Pascarella, E., and Terenzini, P. *How College Affects Students: A Third Decade of Research*. San Francisco: Jossey-Bass, 2005.

Piaget, J. *The Development of Thought: Equilibration of Cognitive Structures* (A. Rosen, Trans.) New York: Viking, 1977.

Rodgers, C. "Defining Reflection: Another Look at John Dewey and Reflective Thinking." *Teachers College Record*, 2002, *104*(4), 842–866.

Rogers, C. *Freedom to Learn*. Columbus, Ohio: Merrill, 1969.

Rogers, C. *On Becoming a Person: A Therapist's View of Psychotherapy*. London: Constable, 1961.

Tavris, C., and Aronson, E. *Mistakes Were Made (But Not by Me): Why We Justify Foolish Beliefs, Bad Decisions, and Hurtful Acts*. Orlando, Fl.: Harcourt, 2007.

Stevens, D. D., and Cooper, J. E. *Journal keeping: How to Use Reflective Writing for Effective Learning, Teaching Professional Insight, and Positive Change*. Sterling, Va.: Stylus, 2009.

DEBORA L. LIDDELL *is associate professor and program coordinator of the Higher Education and Student Affairs Graduate Program at the University of Iowa.*

3

This chapter highlights emerging research and implications for service-learning and moral development. Sections explore questions and considerations, including a reflective planning tool for increasing moral growth opportunities within postsecondary service-learning environments.

The Intersection of Service-Learning and Moral Growth

Joel H. Scott

For the better part of the past 100 years, John Dewey (1916), Ernest Boyer (1987), and other higher education reform advocates have challenged universities to hold true to their civic roots and responsibilities by promoting teaching and scholarship in the context of the real world. In response, service-learning has evolved into a viable pedagogy to encourage deeper learning and development as well as greater personal and social responsibility of students (American Association of Colleges and Universities, 2002, 2006). This chapter describes the components of effective service-learning and emerging research on service-learning and moral development, and poses questions and considerations for increasing moral growth opportunities within service-learning environments.

Understanding Service-Learning

With its roots in moral education and experiential learning (You and Rud, 2010), postsecondary service-learning pedagogy covers a wide variety of disciplines today connecting course assignments, discussions, and written reflections within the context of meaningful community service and real-world problems (National Service-Learning Clearinghouse, 2011). University–community service initiatives have significantly increased over the past two decades as a result of a national call for universities to return to its civic roots (Colby, Elrich, Beaumont, and Stephens, 2003; American Association of Colleges and Universities, 2006). Today, universities encourage student service and community outreach through volunteer initiatives, student organizations, and service-learning while pursuing national civic distinctions such as the Carnegie Community Engagement Classification

NEW DIRECTIONS FOR STUDENT SERVICES, no. 139, Fall 2012 © Wiley Periodicals, Inc.
Published online in Wiley Online Library (wileyonlinelibrary.com) • DOI: 10.1002/ss.20020

(Carnegie Foundation for the Advancement of Teaching, 2011) and the President's Higher Education Honor Roll (National Service-Learning Clearinghouse, 2011). These developments are encouraging in the context of enhancing university–community relationships and supporting service-learning initiatives. Service-learning advocates are quick to caution, however, that service-learning is distinct from courses that require service without regard for course design and learning objectives or university service programs that do not engage in reflection nor connect academic learning in the service context (Eyler and Giles, 1999). This distinction is especially important when considering the degree to which service-learning can evoke deeper learning outcomes, including moral growth. This chapter considers implications for moral growth in the context of a credit bearing service-learning course supported by the context of time (semester or longer), evaluation, and accountability.

Research in Service-Learning and Moral Growth

In their analysis of undergraduate moral growth studies utilizing the Defining Issues Test (DIT), King and Mayhew (2002) affirm the gains in moral judgment related to college participation. King and Mayhew's work supports Pascarella and Terenzini's (2005) extensive analysis of two-plus decades of studies on student learning and development, which affirms that college activity is "linked with statistical increases in the use of principled moral reasoning to judge moral issues" (p. 345). Although specific research on the impact of service-learning and moral growth is still early in its development, there are strong indications that service-learning courses support psychosocial development in areas such as appreciation of diversity, empathy, concern for social justice, and greater sense of personal efficacy and problem solving (Astin, Sax, Ikeda, and Yee, 2000; Bernacki and Jaeger, 2008; Einfeld and Collins, 2008; Marichal, 2010).

Service-learning studies have utilized instruments such as the DIT (Rest, 1986) and the Moral Justification Scales (MJS; Gump, 1994), which measure the degree of moral reasoning and ethic of care and justice used in responding to moral dilemmas. Moral growth has been reported in studies comparing service-learning and non–service-learning courses with larger sample sizes (Boss, 1994; Gorman, Duffy, Heffernan, 1994), while smaller sample studies yield no differences (Green, 1997; Bernacki and Jaeger, 2008). In their excellent analysis, Bernacki and Jaeger (2008) suggest that differences in sample size, age and developmental maturity of participants, and intensity and frequency of service-learning context likely contribute to present moral development variations. High school service experiences, family values, and faith perspectives are also influential factors in students' precollege level of moral development (Scott, 2008). The mixed results in scholarship thus far suggest the need to design quantitative and qualitative mixed method studies that can more holistically describe the complex constructions of moral growth in service-learning (Bernacki and Jaeger, 2008). Despite the mixed results in scholarship, there are important implications from research to consider for service-learning pedagogy and moral growth outcomes.

First, psychosocial growth in curricular and co-curricular experiences supports the total student learning experience in college, including moral growth (Astin, Sax, Ikeda, and Yee, 2000; Pascarella and Terenzini, 2005). Moreover, the positive psychosocial outcomes in service-learning courses provide a rich developmental and cognitive stepping-stone for student moral growth in service-learning experiences (Green, 1997). For example, students who experience an increase in compassion and empathy toward social issues and challenges inherent in service-learning projects may enhance opportunities for moral growth and sophistication (Marichal, 2010). Second, the duration of the service-learning experience and frequency of reflection opportunities during the course are important pedagogical considerations for advancing moral growth (Bernacki and Jaeger, 2008; Eyler and Giles, 1999). Students of service-learning who are required to consistently engage in a service-learning project over the course of a semester or longer will likely take more ownership of their learning and embrace the struggles they may encounter in their service projects, community challenges, peer differences, and the like. If students are challenged to critically process and reflect on experiences in the real-world context on a consistent basis, it is more likely that they will encounter the cognitive dissonance needed to activate moral growth (Kohlberg, 1971). The next section responds to three pragmatic questions and considerations related to service-learning course design and moral growth opportunities:

1. How can service-learning use good learning practices, such as reflection, to facilitate growth?
2. How should service-learning be evaluated when it is so focused on process and outcomes may not be immediately realized?
3. How can service-learning cultivate relationships that lead to moral growth?

How Can Service-Learning Use Good Learning Practices to Facilitate Moral Growth?: Integrating a Reflective Planning Tool for Moral Growth

Good practices in service-learning within the literature all point toward the importance of intentional reflection (Marichal, 2010; You and Rud, 2010). But what does service-learning reflection that encourages moral growth look like? Reflections that evoke moral growth must go beyond the transfer of basic knowledge or recollection of activities. Written or dialogical reflections need to evoke a sense of struggle in feelings, viewpoints, and tensions necessary to expand moral reasoning and development (Kohlberg, 1971;

Rest, 1986). Service-learning courses that intersect academic learning in the context of relevant community partnerships are potentially rich opportunities for students to wrestle with moral-related issues through consistent and challenging yet supportive reflection and dialogue. Unfortunately, few resources or models exist to assist faculty and student affairs professionals with service-learning questions that progressively evoke moral development throughout the different stages of a service-learning course.

Rest's (1986) framework of moral growth, supported by authors of this book, is a germane resource for exploring how reflection in service-learning intersects with his four dimensions of moral maturity: moral sensitivity, judgment, motivation, and character. While Rest's framework is considered fluid and dynamic, and should not be viewed as rigidly sequential, this sequencing is beneficial to understanding student growth. Based on this framework, it is in these experiences that students build relationships, struggle with social issues, and move toward self-authorship. The intent of this reflective planning tool is to provide a possible map of potential intersections between experiences and reflections through the progression of a semester-long service-learning course. The tool is also a reflection of my observations and experiences as a service-learning instructor and ardent supporter of learner-centered theories, which focus on creating learning environments that encourage a community of learning and self-authorship (Baxter Magolda, 2001). Rather than acting as "banks of knowledge," service-learning instructors facilitate thoughtful questions and assignments that evoke shared learning, empowerment, and responsibility (Freire, 2000). The series of example questions within this reflective tool is also grounded in the growing recognition of the importance of ontology and meaning making in moral growth (Marichal, 2010) guiding individuals toward greater self-awareness and analysis. For an overview of the intersection of moral growth dimensions with service-learning experiences, reflection, and stages of development in service-learning, see Table 3.1.

Moral Sensitivity in Service-Learning. The first component of the Rest framework is moral sensitivity. Moral sensitivity emerges in service-learning as students are exposed to the community and begin to identify conflicts and challenges facing local communities or practices that diverge from their own moral codes. This recognition may lead to personal insecurities or discomfort with their service environment. It is always striking to me how many traditional-age college students today may be experiencing "firsts" in service environments. Service-learning educators should be cautious in presuming what incoming traditional-age students should have already experienced in their communities prior to college, despite the national reports on increased service activity (Higher Education Research Institute, 2006). These first-time encounters represent a great opportunity to morally capitalize on the early tensions students may experience related to moral sensitivity. In addition to processing the very real encounters students experience in their community engagement, role playing with

Table 3.1. Overview of Intersection of Moral Growth Dimensions, Service-Learning Experiences, Reflection, and Service-Learning Stages

Rest's Moral Growth Dimensions	Intersection of Service-Learning Experiences and Moral Growth Dimension	Reflective Question Example	Service-Learning Stages of Development
Moral Sensitivity	Service environment observations, empathy, compassion, first-time exposure (insecurity, fears), awareness of socioeconomic, race, or religious differences	What about your community engagement has been eye-opening?	Early: Building relationships, understanding of service environment
Moral Judgment	Constructive thinking and recognition of organizational systems, pluralism, social issues, worldview differences	How do you see institutional structures impacting the people at your community engagement site?	Early to Middle: Increased investment in relationships
Moral Motivation	Processing conflicting or competing values; identification and development of beliefs, passions, convictions, and action(s)	What's more important right now if you had to choose: being just or being fair?	Middle to End: High investment in relationships and commitment
Moral Character	Increased self-understanding and evaluation; synergy between values and actions resulting in integrity	How are your values expressed through your community engagement?	Middle to End: High investment in relationships and commitment to personal and intrapersonal growth

different perspectives in the classroom, for example, can also stimulate reflections on topics related to moral sensitivity, such as empathy, compassion, feelings of inadequacy or efficacy, and sensitivity to cultural differences. Student reflections should be facilitated in a variety of ways: journaling, small-group discussions and debates, in-class one-minute-message responses, and self-awareness assessments in written format. The traditional approach of journaling is appropriate but should be strengthened by providing timely prompts that evoke critical reflection and normalize dissonance. Example questions designed to encourage moral sensitivity in a variety of service-learning courses are presented next.

NEW DIRECTIONS FOR STUDENT SERVICES • DOI: 10.1002/ss

- Describe what feelings or thoughts you are having as you adapt to your new service environment. What surprises you, and why? What were you expecting that you did or didn't see?
- In what ways are you comfortable in your service experience? In what ways are you uncomfortable?
- Describe any new observation(s) about a person or human behavior that is connected to your experiences in your service-learning environment experience.
- How are resources (for example, leadership, time, money, power) distributed in the setting of your service?

Early exposure moments are fertile for supporting students to articulate their feelings and reactions to the service environment, people, and processes.

Moral Judgment in Service-Learning. When students invest in their service setting, people, or projects, they often are quick to offer solutions to problems they observe or experience. For example, I often observe students who tutor at-risk children generously offer solutions for how parents or teachers can increase learning and development for their tutees. Their written reflections and classroom discussions are emotive. As students wrestle with concepts of leadership in education, they focus on helping the children. Student development theories are helpful here in understanding how traditional-age students think and feel about challenges faced in service-learning. For instance, students who encounter injustices in service may be more likely to describe dilemmas as "black and white" or "right or wrong" rather than as tensions and contradictions (Chickering and Reisser, 1993). Students' eagerness to right the wrongs they see in public education and other systems creates fertile ground for stirring moral growth.

Moral judgment or reasoning encompasses a struggle to discern a course of action to take that is just and fair (Rest, Narvaez, Bebeau, and Thoma, 1999). Reflective questions should challenge a greater sense of struggle with moral judgment and focus on principles rather than simply right-or-wrong rationales to justify a proposed plan of action. Moral judgment questions also include ethical conflicts, recognition of pluralism, and social justice—all of which can be further stimulated through group projects. As students learn about community needs and negotiate a response and course of action, they benefit by recognizing the complexities related to moral judgment. The next questions can help students acknowledge their worldviews and assumptions.

- In what ways can systems of service perpetuate the very injustices they are trying to eliminate?
- How can the theories and concepts presented in class apply in the context of your service environment? What gaps exist?

- While engaged in your project, what have you observed or experienced that has challenged your worldview?
- Describe justice. What does justice look like in this community partnership?

Moral Motivation in Service-Learning. Moral motivation involves the cognitive struggle of identifying and prioritizing moral values that motivate a course of action. The more an individual identifies with a moral value or values, the more likely he or she is to act (Rest, Narvaez, Bebeau, and Thoma, 1999). A quality service-learning experience exposes students to competing values. Collaborative assignments focus on responses to community needs and challenges and provide students with opportunities to struggle with moral motivation. The next questions can further build student capacity for meaning making and authorship of their moral values as it relates to action.

- Describe a few absolute truths or values in your life right now. How do these truths motivate you to act in a socially just and responsible manner?
- How do you approach discerning between doing what is "right" versus "more right" for others?
- How do you respond right now to viewpoints with which you disagree or that make you feel uncomfortable?
- What theories introduced in this class align with or are in conflict with your values? What is the conflict about?

Moral Character in Service-Learning. In this stage of moral growth, students exemplify the courage, integrity, and persistence to act on the determined course of moral action. Character development—especially across the liberal arts curriculum—is a long-espoused objective in higher education. It is a pedagogy based on experiential learning. Active learning efforts, such as service-learning, provide spaces for students to introspectively reflect on their developing values, convictions, and actions that contribute to the lifelong process of developing character (Strain, 2005). Questions focus on identity and integrity in the context of the later stages of the service-learning course experience. The next questions challenge students to make evaluative connections between who they are becoming.

- In what ways, if any, have you evolved in your thinking this year? Provide specific examples and detailed descriptions.
- To what degree do you believe your beliefs and actions are synergistic? What needs adjustment? What needs further sharpening?
- On a scale from 1 to 10 (10 being extremely comfortable), rank your comfort level during your service-learning experience this year.

NEW DIRECTIONS FOR STUDENT SERVICES • DOI: 10.1002/ss

Provide examples of when you felt most comfortable and uncomfortable.
- Can a person do "good" for the community if he or she is not morally considered a "good person"? Why or why not?

How Should Service-Learning Be Evaluated?

Identifying moral growth opportunities at different stages of service-learning is an important step in addressing the second question of this chapter: How should service-learning be evaluated when it is so focused on process and outcomes may be in the distance? One of the strengths of service-learning is the subjective process, the important moments where students construct meaningful connections (Marichal, 2010) between experiences in the service field and academic learning. By integrating thoughtful and morally provocative questions in concert with anticipated service-learning stages, as demonstrated in the previous section, an instructor can build related learning objectives into the curriculum from the outset. Rest's moral dimensions serve as four learning targets to create measurable outcomes in a variety of service-learning courses. For example, evidences of learning in moral sensitivity include outcomes such as ability to differentiate between personal and community beliefs, articulate meaningful connections and differences between empathy and justice, or reflectively demonstrate concern for community members. Each one of the moral components discussed throughout this volume can assist instructors in identifying learning outcomes that uniquely fit the service and academic environment.

Critical to designing outcomes that drive the learning experience is integrating tools to help evaluate reflective assignments and activities. Rubrics are a practical tool to assess learning outcomes in written and oral assignments. Rubrics bring focus, documentation, and a healthy balance of objective measurement and qualitative attention to the subjective nature of learning (Schuh and Upcraft, 2001). The American Association of Colleges and Universities recently designed a series of research-based Value Rubrics to assist faculty in the creation and evaluation of personal and social responsibility and related moral outcomes (Rhodes, 2010). The series is organized into a values framework with rich descriptions and expectations for each related learning outcome. Service-learning faculty members can utilize this timely resource for course and assignment construction to enhance opportunities for moral learning. Once learning outcomes are established and corresponding assignments are created for my courses, I integrate the outcomes into a rubric designed to quantitatively rank outcomes supplemented by constructive feedback. Having a series of rubrics for individual and group assignments has allowed me to understand more holistically where moral learning and development is at play and, perhaps more important, where it is not. Rubrics provide instructors with a mixed method approach to focus moral growth moments during the process of service-learning and provide specific documentation of outcome efforts and efficacy.

How Can Service-Learning Cultivate Relationships That Lead to Moral Growth?

The third and final question for exploring the intersection of service-learning and moral growth focuses on the importance of human relationships. Specifically, how can service-learning cultivate relationships that lead to moral growth? The dissonance that often occurs in advancing moral growth is ideally situated in a service-learning course grounded in relationships. A review of the moral dimensions explored in this volume highlights the potential for moral growth in the context of service-learning relationships. A college student, for example, who becomes emotionally invested in an elementary school student he is tutoring in a service-learning course is much more likely to morally struggle with the social conditions impacting public school education because of his developing relationship(s) than a student who only creates a resource for the school apart from engaging with students and administrators. Potential for effective relationships in service-learning requires several considerations.

First, it is much easier to cultivate relationships if the partnership involves interacting directly with community members and encourages consistent engagement. The past several years, I have witnessed significant differences in my students' level of moral engagement in courses that expect weekly service-learning involvement than in courses focused on total hours of service without regard for relationship or consistency. This observation is congruent with research that highlights the importance of time and intensity in service and moral growth (Bernacki and Jaeger, 2008).

Second, I strongly encourage faculty to assign coursework requiring students to work together in the context of the community. Working collaboratively with other students not only encourages relational investment but also provides opportunities for working through peer conflicts and differences, which open the doors further for moral dissonance and growth. Third, faculty members set the tone for the importance of relationships in service-learning. It is difficult to implement a service-learning partnership if the instructor has little involvement with the community agency or members involved. Students, I contend, respond accordingly to the degree of relational connection faculty members have developed with the community being served. Moreover, if faculty expectations for building relationships and consistent engagement are not established early in the service-learning course, the potential for moral sensitivity, awareness, and empathy often encountered when students make relational connections with community members and peers may be limited. Even worse, when service-learning is engaged in outside the context of relationship, the course may simply provide students with another opportunity to experience learning as a consumptive activity and service as a resume builder (Scott, 2008).

Important Caveats and Reminders

Exploring pedagogical techniques to encourage moral growth in service-learning requires careful attention to supporting student development (Chickering and Reisser, 1993). Perry (1999) and other cognitive development scholars contend that if students are pushed too far without faculty support, they often retreat from this transformative opportunity. In this fight-or-flight moment, students may actually withdraw to a more comfortable intellectual place of self-preservation. Instructors should be cognizant of the power differential with students and be able to show discretion in our responses and reactions to morally sensitive situations, discussions, and reflections, especially with students who are only seeking instructor or peer approval.

Crafting reflective questions for moral learning requires practice and trust in the learning community. Even seasoned facilitators find that processing morally sensitive conversations and reflections is challenging. The good news is that there is no better preparation for improving our skills as facilitators of moral growth than to try it and to learn from our mistakes. Be prepared as well to be challenged by student viewpoints and open to allowing the service-learning experiences to challenge your own moral maturity.

Finally, creating a quality service learning course is challenging, especially if one of the goals is to heighten student moral growth. Time will be needed to develop a mutually beneficial community partnership. Doing this requires interviewing to gauge the potential for a relationship that is based on mutuality, respect, interest, and sustainability. Moreover, I believe it is incumbent on the instructor to set the tone for a quality service-learning partnership, which requires thinking about the kind of service and academic learning that is desired before interviewing a community partner. Attention should be given to a dynamic syllabus that outlines the expectations, accountability, and evaluation of the service, including thoughtful consideration of individual reflections and group assignments as they connect with anticipated moral learning objectives. Courses that connect learning inside and outside the classroom require more faculty involvement and coordination than traditional courses and therefore require a great deal of preparation.

Closing Thoughts

This chapter highlights how Rest's four moral dimensions can serve as a map for understanding the intersection of service-learning reflection and moral growth opportunities. A reflective planning tool, such as the one presented in this chapter, can cultivate constructive dialogue and written reflections that heighten moral thinking and learning. Timely and thoughtful questions based on moral sensitivity, judgment, motivation, and character highlight the course of a relationally intensive service-learning experience.

References

Association of American Colleges and Universities. *Greater Expectations: A New Vision for Learning as a Nation Prepares to go to College.* Washington, D.C.: Association of American Colleges and Universities, 2002.

Association of American Colleges and Universities. "AAC&U Announces National Initiative on Fostering Personal and Social Responsibility in Today's College Students." 2006. Retrieved September 30, 2007, from http://www.aacu.org/press_room/press_releases/index.cfm.

Astin, A. W., Sax, L. J., Ikeda, E. K., and Yee, J. A. "Executive Summary: How Service Learning Affects Students." Los Angeles: Graduate School of Education and Information Studies, University of California-Los Angeles, 2000.

Baxter Magolda, M. B. *Making Their Own Way: Narratives for Transforming Higher Education to Promote Self-Development.* Sterling, Va.: Stylus, 2001.

Bernacki, M. L., and Jaeger, E. "Exploring the Impact of Service-Learning on Moral Development and Moral Orientation." *Michigan Journal of Community Service Learning*, 2008, *14*(2), 5–15.

Boss, J. A. "The Effect of Community Service on the Moral Development of College Ethics Students." *Journal of Moral Education*, 1994, *23*(2), 183–198.

Boyer, E. L. *College: The Undergraduate Experience in America.* New York: HarperCollins, 1987.

Carnegie Foundation for the Advancement of Teaching. "Community Engagement Elective Classification." 2011. Retrieved November 20, 2011, from http://www.carnegiefoundation.org/.

Chickering, A. W., and Reisser, L. *Education and Identity*, 2nd ed. San Francisco: Jossey-Bass, 1993.

Colby, A., Elrich, T., Beaumont, E., and Stephens, J. *Educating Citizens: Preparing America's Undergraduates for Lives of Moral and Civic Responsibility.* San Francisco: Jossey-Bass, 2003.

Dewey, J. *Democracy and Education: An Introduction to the Philosophy of Education.* New York: Macmillan, 1916.

Einfeld, A., and Collins, D. "The Relationship Between Service-Learning, Social Justice, Multicultural Competence, and Civic Engagement." *Journal of College Student Development*, 2008, *49*(2), 95–109.

Eyler. J. S., and Giles, D. E. *Where's the Learning in Service Learning?* San Francisco: Jossey-Bass, 1999.

Freire, P. *The Pedagogy of the Oppressed* (30th anniversary edition). New York: Continuum, 2000.

Gorman, M., Duffy, J., and Heffernan, M. "Service Experience and the Moral Development of College Students." *Religious Education*, 1994, *89*(3), 422–431.

Green, D. "The Use of Service-Learning in Client Environments to Enhance Ethical Reasoning in Students." *American Journal of Occupational Therapy*, 1997, *51*(10), 844–852.

Gump, L. S. "The Relationship of Culture and Gender to Moral Decision-Making." Unpublished doctoral dissertation, California School of Professional Psychology, 1994.

Higher Education Research Institute. *The American Freshman: National Norms for Fall 2006.* Los Angeles: Higher Education Research Institute, University of California-Los Angeles, 2006.

King, P., and Mayhew, M. "Moral Judgment Development in Higher Education: Insights from the Defining Issues Test." *Journal of Moral Education,* 2002, *31*(3), 247–270.

Kohlberg, L. *Philosophy of Moral Education.* New York: Harper & Row, 1971.

Marichal, J. "You Call This Service? A Civic Ontology Approach to Evaluating Service-Learning in Diverse Communities." *Journal of Political Science Education,* 2010, *6*(2), 142–162.

National Service-Learning Clearinghouse. "What Is Learn and Serve America?" 2011. Retrieved November 20, 2011, from http://www.learnandserve.gov/about/lsa/index.asp.

Pascarella, E. T., and Terenzini, P. *How Colleges Affect Students: A Third Decade of Research.* San Francisco: Jossey-Bass, 2005.

Perry, W. G. *Forms of Intellectual and Ethical Development in the College Years: A Scheme.* San Francisco: Jossey-Bass, 1999.

Rest, J. *Manual for the Defining Issues Test,* 3rd ed. Minneapolis: University of Minnesota Center for the Study of Ethical Development, 1986.

Rest, J., Narvaez, D., Bebeau, M., and Thoma, S. *Post-Conventional Moral Thinking: A Neo-Kohlbergian Approach.* Mahwah, N.J.: Lawrence Erlbaum, 1999.

Rhodes, T. (ed.). *Assessing Outcomes and Improving Achievement: Tips and Tools for Using Rubrics.* Washington, D.C.: Association of American Colleges and Universities, 2010.

Schuh, J. H., and Upcraft, M. L. *Assessment Practice in Student Affairs: An Applications Manual.* San Francisco: Jossey-Bass, 2001.

Scott, J. H. "Exploring Institutional Culture and Student Civic Engagement: A Constructivist Inquiry." Unpublished doctoral dissertation, Department of Counseling and Human Development, University of Georgia, 2008.

Strain, C. R. "Pedagogy and Practice: Service-Learning and Students' Moral Development." In N. S. Leff (ed.), *Identity, Learning, and the Liberal Arts.* New Directions for Teaching and Learning, no. 103. San Francisco: Jossey-Bass, 2005.

You, Z., and Rud, A. G. "A Model of Dewey's Moral Imagination for Service Learning: Theoretical Explorations and Implications for Practice in Higher Education." *Education and Culture,* 2010, *26*(2), 36–51.

JOEL H. SCOTT is a clinical assistant professor in higher education administration at Boston University.

NEW DIRECTIONS FOR STUDENT SERVICES • DOI: 10.1002/ss

This chapter explores the components of civic engagement with the ultimate goal of increasing personal and social responsibility.

Promoting Civic Engagement to Educate Institutionally for Personal and Social Responsibility

Karen D. Boyd, Sarah Brackmann

A democratic system of government needs—and the United States relies on colleges to produce—ethical and engaged citizens. A society will be able to sustain and flourish by cultivating civic engagement while equally developing a moral compass along with the ability and will to act (Hersh and Schneider, 2005). Historically colleges have and can continue to maximize students' civic engagement and ethical learning when both are envisioned as integrated goals straddling students' academic and nonacademic lives and permeating institutional culture (Rudolph, 1962; Colby, Ehrlich, Beaumont, and Corngold, 2007; Jacoby, 2009). A pervasive, intertwined, and intentional approach to encouraging civic engagement with an acknowledged moral dimension enhances the development of personal and social responsibility (PSR) in students (Chickering, 2001; Swaner, 2004, 2005; Pascarella and Terenzini, 2005).This chapter examines the mechanisms, best practices, administrative considerations, and resources available for *institutionally* promoting civic engagement activity as an educational tool designed to facilitate moral growth and a civic mind-set (for example, attitudes and values).

The theory of postconventional moral thinking (Rest, Narvaez, Bebeau, and Thoma, 1999) demonstrates the educational value of a comprehensive universitywide promotion of civic engagement in facilitating personal and social reasonable action. As the frequency and intensity of involvement in public service increases, so will students' exposure to and consideration of others' perspectives increase. Students' moral sensitivity and judgment/reasoning—Rest's first and second frames of moral

NEW DIRECTIONS FOR STUDENT SERVICES, no. 139, Fall 2012 © Wiley Periodicals, Inc.
Published online in Wiley Online Library (wileyonlinelibrary.com) • DOI: 10.1002/ss.20021

maturity—develop as students engage in real-world problem solving and civic activities that expand their ability to take another's perspective and their level of empathy toward that perspective. Additionally, engaging in civic activities is an ethical behavior. Frequent participation in these perspective-expanding experiences develops in students an identity of and commitment toward continuing similar ethical conduct—Rest's third component of moral maturity, moral motivation. Last, civic engagement activities typically provide the supportive environment and experienced guides needed to support and facilitate a student's ethical and effective actions. These interactions encourage a student's moral character, Rest's fourth component of moral maturity.

Civic Engagement

The term "civic engagement" is often imprecisely bundled or used interchangeably with experiential civic education strategies such as service-learning, community engagement, volunteerism, public scholarship, community service, and other strategies connecting higher education with the public good (Saltmarsh, 2005). There is some consensus that, minimally, civic engagement is participation in political or community affairs (Carnegie Foundation for the Advancement of Teaching, 2006) and that the objectives of civic learning, the "development of a capacity for engagement" (Saltmarsh, 2005, p. 50), include civic and moral knowledge, skills, and values. Civic engagement is both a pedagogical strategy and an outcome of participating in these activities.

Confusion often arises from the operationalization of the definition. The terms "civic engagement" and "community engagement" are also seen as synonymous, although community engagement encompasses a much broader application of higher education's resources to society's problems. Also, there is some hesitation to consider service to or engagement in the life of the college as civic engagement, yet the civic engagement scholarship—most predominantly the Wingspread Declaration on Campus Compact (Boyte and Hollander, 1999) and the Circle initiative (Carnegie Foundation for the Advancement of Teaching, 2006)—is clear that student participation in communities both on and off campus are hallmarks of collegiate civic engagement.

Institutional Exemplar: Coalition for Civic Engagement and Leadership

Civic engagement initiatives need to become less about "effective educational strategies [and more about] ... learning outcomes that have a civic dimension" (Saltmarsh, 2005, p. 55). Yet few campuses have developed concrete comprehensive strategic plans for delivering and maximizing the learning potential of civic engagement activities (Carnegie Foundation for the Advancement of Teaching, 2006).

An exemplar institutional civic engagement program with an ethical dimension is the University of Maryland's Coalition for Civic Engagement and Leadership (Adams-Gaston, Jacoby, and Peres, 2005). Its working definition of civic engagement is:

> acting upon a heightened sense of responsibility to one's communities. This includes a wide range of activities, including developing civic sensitivity, participation in building civil society, and benefiting the common good.
>
> Civic engagement encompasses the notions of global citizenship and interdependence. Through civic engagement, individuals—as citizens of their communities, their nations, and the world—are empowered as agents of positive social change for a more democratic world [p. 2].

This chapter conceptualizes civic engagement as "working to make a difference in the civic life of [all of] our communities and developing the combination of [Rest's moral] knowledge, skills, value, and motivation to make that difference" (Erlich, 2000, p. vi). This definition suggests that civic engagement can be both an indicator and a measure of PSR and a strategy for contributing to PSR learning (Musil, 2009).

Educating for Personal and Social Responsibility

Colleges and universities should take the lead in creating intentional environments which will promote personally and socially responsible graduates.

PSR Defined. PSR has emerged as one of higher education's "essential learning outcomes" (Association of American Colleges and Universities [AAC&U], 2007, p. 3). AAC&U's Liberal Education and America's Promise (LEAP) (2007) project has encouraged a national dialogue with the faculty and administrators of colleges and universities on one hand and the business community on the other. Instead of proposing a finite definition for PSR, AAC&U's Core Commitments: Educating for PSR project (n.d.) explained the construct using five dimensions:

1. *Striving for excellence.* Developing a strong work ethic and consciously doing one's very best in all aspects of college
2. *Cultivating personal and academic integrity.* Recognizing and acting on a sense of honor, ranging from honesty in relationships to principled engagement with a formal academic honor code
3. *Contributing to a larger community.* Recognizing and acting on one's responsibility to the educational community (classroom, campus life), the local community, and the wider society, both national and global
4. *Taking seriously the perspectives of others.* Recognizing and acting on the obligation to inform one's own judgment; engaging diverse and

competing perspectives as a resource for learning, for citizenship, and for work

5. *Developing competence in ethical and moral reasoning.* Developing one's own personal and social values and being able to express and act upon those values responsibly; developing a mature sense of moral sensitivity and personal character; being able to identify and evaluate moral dilemmas and act appropriately [AAC&U, n.d., p. 2].

This construct proposed a new integrative way of thinking about "values, character, ethical challenges, and/or social justice" (Hersh and Schneider, 2005, p. 8) and educational outcomes (AAC&U, n.d.). The principles of civic engagement permeate these dimensions, suggesting a return in some respects to higher education's original pedagogical paradigm (Newman, 1985).

Mutually Reinforcing Metacurricular Constructs

Civic education is an aspect of educating for PSR (Musil, 2009). Therefore, addressing educating for PSR equates to educating for citizenship (Colby and Sullivan, 2009).

Theoretical Context. Advances in moral development research have validated significant elements of the historical approach to educating for PSR. The cultivation of moral growth and promotion of civic engagement are interdependent activities with multiple overlapping elements (Colby and others, 2003; Adams-Gaston and others, 2005) and most effective if infused throughout the collegiate experience (Colby and Ehrlich, n.d.). Moral growth is a combination of cognitive and affective processes (Swaner, 2004). These processes expand one's perspective increasingly outward, moving away from self-centered decision making to consideration of others less closely related to the individual and their self-interest (Kohlberg, 1981, 1984; Perry, 1999). The range of civic engagement activities provides plus-one interventions—meaning interventions that challenge students with moral thinking one level of moral development above their current state—that can be arranged across enrollment to move students farther and farther away from self-centric thinking. Additionally, the exposure to challenges others face that students experience during civic engagement activities promotes empathy, which is a motivator for moral action in students (Foubert and Newberry, 2006).

Associational Exemplar: Core Commitment Project. Depending heavily on this theoretical base to shape its research assumptions and agenda, AAC&U (2006) launched the Core Commitments project. This associational exemplar program revitalized the notion that educating for PSR and civic engagement are interdependent goals while retaining a commitment to implementing metacurricular processes to achieve these outcomes (Swaner, 2004, 2005; Hersh and Schneider, 2005). AAC&U selected 23 best practice campuses to join the research consortium. Teams of faculty, staff, and administrators set out to intentionally provide "mutually reinforcing academic, interpersonal, and extracurricular involvements" (Pascarella and Terenzini, 2005, p. 647). Institutions committed to pursue and assess a "holistic" (Pascarella and Terenzini, 2005, p. 646), integrated set of institution-wide learning outcomes of and antecedents to continued civic engagement (Musil, 2009) and moral growth (Swaner, 2004, 2005).

The stated purpose of the Core Commitments: Educating Students for Personal and Social Responsibility (PSR) project was to ignite and support college's efforts to encourage students to examine, develop, and personalize their integrity, excellence, ethical and moral reasoning capabilities, contribution to the larger community (civic engagement), and ability to take seriously the perspective of others (that is, empathy) (Association of American Colleges and Universities, n.d.). By facilitating empirically grounded research on PSR education, AAC&U seeks to support and increase the intentional production of civically and morally competent, responsible, and engaged citizens by colleges and universities.

Leading researchers in moral development and campus life—including the Astins, Bebeau, Hurtado, and Knefelkamp—conceptualized the best indicators of PSR (dimensions) and identified what colleges could do to facilitate PSR education (Association of American Colleges and Universities, 2004). A primary focus of the Core Commitments project was to develop and analyze assessment data. To facilitate institutional assessment efforts, the team examined student, faculty, and administrator perceptions of the impact of curricular and teaching strategies (Personal and Social Responsibility Institutional Inventory [PSRII]), developed a self-assessment cultural audit to identify the prevalence of PSR activities on campus, and disseminated the Values Rubrics as a tool to assess progress on learning outcomes (Swaner, 2004, 2005; Hersh and Schneider, 2005).

PSR-Promoting Civic Engagement Activities and Initiatives

Colleges are engaged in PSR education, whether they have fully embraced their role in its promotion or not. Infusion of service-learning into the curriculum is a key strategy in institutional efforts to impact students' level of civic engagement and moral growth. However, service-learning, because of its focus on curricular content, is limited in its impact as a tool for PSR education. To be effective, PSR education must include the classroom, but to maximize institutional effectiveness, initiatives should include other PSR-producing engagement experiences.

For the purposes of this discussion, we focus on metacurricular civic engagement pedagogies independent, yet reinforcing, of curricular content. We classify these student affairs practitioner-driven activities or partnering opportunities into five categories, including campus culture and environmental initiatives, structured civic discourse/dialogue, on-campus civic leadership, student protest and issue advocacy, and political engagement.

Creating Campus Culture as Community. Campus culture embodies Rest, Narvaez, Bebeau, and Thoma's (1999) concept of macro-morality. "Academic, interpersonal, and extracurricular involvements are mutually reinforcing" (Pascarella and Terenzini, 2005, p. 646) and produce the greatest impact on student learning if understood as and intentionally used in integrated and "holistic rather than segmented" (p. 647) approaches to achieve institutionwide educational outcomes in general.

Currently, most environmentally focused ethics initiatives rely on institutional messaging to create an ethos of PSR on campus (Colby, Ehrlich, Beaumont, and Stephens, 2003). The increased levels of academic honesty found at Academic Honor Code schools exemplify the power of environmental intervention for educating for PSR (McCabe, 2005; McCabe and Trevino, 1993, 1996; McCabe, Trevino, and Butterfield, 1999). This concept is further developed and discussed in Chapter Five. Institutional messages associated with honor systems communicate an undiluted statement of students' civic responsibility for and an institutional commitment to the academic integrity of the college.

Student development scholars have suggested that the relationship between the student and the institution is really a matter of the interaction of the person and environment (as in Student-Institution Relationship $= f$ ([*Person* $\times$ *Environment*]) (Banning, 1978; Miller and others, 2005). The quality of the relationship or climate is believed to influence students' learning and action. Most notably, Boyer (Carnegie Foundation, 1990) conceptualized the student–institution relationship as community with relational qualities. He proposed that colleges hoping to positively impact students personally and in socially responsible behavior be communities with purposeful, open, just, disciplined, caring, and celebrative qualities. Environments ultimately are able to promote student involvement and engagement if students feel a sense of connectedness, belonging, and mattering to the educational institution (Strange and Banning, 2001; Libbey, 2004; Loukas, Suzuki, and Horton, 2006). For example, institutional policies allowing for student conduct processes that are interpersonally driven, when appropriate, such as restorative justice and other conflict resolution processes, reflect these qualities and attend to students' affective needs. Interventions that institutionally address these relational quality goals intentionally contour student experiences to increase the likelihood of student learning (Strange and Banning, 2001; Boyd and Cooper, 2008; Boyd, 2010).

Environmental press, defined as the characteristic pressures and influences of the campus culture toward conformity (Pace and Stern, 1958), when combined with clear institutional messaging and a conducive institutional climate, can be an effective means of creating a civic engagement and ethical identity and motivation in college community members (Rest, Narvaez, Bebeau, and Thoma, 1999). Campuses should identify and intentionally use elements of their unique campus culture and environment combined with selected programmatic activities, such as the next examples, to develop comprehensive strategic learning-oriented action plans that influence students' engagement and PSR behavior and learning.

Structured Civic Discourse–Dialogue. The ability to participate in civic discourse and dialogue that shares differing perspectives and brainstorms possible responses is a necessary skill for ethical reasoning (Carnegie Foundation for the Advancement of Teaching, 2006) and an important component of a liberal education. Similar to Kohlberg's (1981, 1984) just community, colleges and universities can help to foster these skills through structured forums focusing on political, social, and economic topics affecting them and their communities. Civic conversations allow students to practice reasoning, consider diverse opinions and perspectives, formulate unbiased and logical arguments, and engage in civil and respectful discussion. Civic discourse can be as informal as Carnegie Mellon University's faculty conversations with residence hall students about the big questions facing society to more formal conversations requiring increasing levels of organization, staff effort, and training to implement.

On-Campus Civic Leadership. Few campuses recognize the civic engagement dimensions of on-campus service, and so they are not intentionally shaping these experiences for maximum benefit. Service to the campus can be a powerful civic engagement experience and can effectively educate for PSR for a number of reasons, not the least of which is the immediate and intensely personal impact of these activities on students. Additionally, on-campus civic leadership—orientation, ambassadors, tour guides, student government, conduct boards, and peer advisors and educators (resident advisors, counseling, health, and Greek new member educators)—activates the moral development process of social role taking. In social role taking, both student leaders and those with whom they interact benefit from these activities in that the leaders embrace the institutional message they are conveying while the recipients are more likely to accept the message from peers (Sprinthall and Scott, 1989). Social role taking takes effect only if there is a focus on the ethical and civic dimension and only if the student engages in active reflection. Therefore, for these experiences to have a PSR impact, they must be shaped to do so.

Student Protests and Issue Activism. Not all civic engagement activities are welcomed by college and university administration or local communities. Student protest and issue advocacy can be disruptive on a college campus. Be it civil rights sit-ins, cardboard shanties protesting apartheid, alcohol riots, G-20 protest rallies, tuition or other campus policy protest, or Occupy movements, the potential for missed classes, property and human injury, criminal records, and diversion of scarce campus resources is present. However, desired learning outcomes—Kohlberg's

(1981, 1984) principled level of moral judgment (Nassi, 1981) and human-itarianism (Rosas, 2010)—are also higher in activists. Student affairs prac-titioners are challenged with finding strategies that permit the growth opportunities inherent in the freedom of expression while also maintaining an academic environment conducive to other learning. An example of this approach would be the observer program developed at the University of California at Berkeley, designed to protect protester rights while accu-rately chronicling the events surrounding student protest. Student peers, faculty, and staff are trained to be silent witnesses (that is, observe and report) to events impacting the campus. Additionally, these programs assist protesters in dissenting within reasonable societal boundaries. The observer program and other similar policies allow campuses to balance academic freedom, protect campus civility, and maintain relationships with all students.

Political Engagement. Students' political participation ranges from low-commitment activities, such as joining a political party student organi-zation, to high-commitment activities, such as hosting a political fund-raiser or candidate on campus. Political engagement suggests the action of political participation but also the development of political skills, motiva-tion, and political efficacy to understand students' role in the political pro-cess. A common political engagement strategy involves the organization of voter registration drives. Campus Compact (www.compact.org), Rock the Vote (MTV) (www.rockthevote.com), and Project Vote (projectvote.org) provide strategies, resources, and ongoing and election season activities for college students to utilize for election education and registration.

Considerations for Developing Model Metacurricular Programs

From this patchwork of theoretical knowledge and institutional approaches, practitioners can develop core ideas to inform the creation of the programmatic aspects of a PSR metacurriculum. Given that educating for PSR is a learning endeavor first and foremost (Boyd and Cooper, 2008), and civic engagement is a dimension of PSR, administrators organizing institutional PSR initiatives should take the Documenting Effective Educa-tional Practices (DEEP) ideas into consideration. These six conditions, found to be common to each of the DEEP schools, provide guidance for organizing an institutionwide PSR-promoting civic engagement framework (Kuh and others, 2005):

1. *"Living" mission and "lived" educational philosophy.* Be intentional.
2. *Unshakable focus on student learning.* Be integrative and informed.
3. *Environments adapted for educational enrichment.* Be innovative.
4. *Clearly marked pathways to student success.* Be intentional.
5. *Improvement-oriented ethos.* Be increasingly better.
6. *Shared responsibility.* Be inclusive and supportive.

NEW DIRECTIONS FOR STUDENT SERVICES • DOI: 10.1002/ss

Overcoming the Barriers

Dissatisfaction on the part of higher education and society at large with regard to the outcomes of a college education and students' misbehaviors drove an intentional effort on the part of colleges to develop students' ethical decision-making abilities and contributions to the community. However, not all members of the academic community embrace AAC&U's commitment to educating students for PSR. The fundamental challenge is that in a culture dedicated to academic freedom, some have a sincere philosophical concern that educating for PSR through civic engagement is actually an enculturation of values. Coordination of a metacurricular goal without a curricular home or significant academic partnership and buy-in relegates the initiative to a secondary status. Armed with an awareness of these challenges, practitioners have the knowledge to shape action plans for implementing initiatives that proactively address these concerns.

As a whole, the higher education community recognizes and is coming to accept society's long-held expectation that educating for PSR is a core commitment of colleges and universities (Association of American Colleges and Universities, n.d.). Students' civic engagement activities can promote moral development and growth. The campus culture and environment, structured civic discourse/dialogue, on-campus civic leadership, student protest and issue advocacy, and political engagement provide opportunities for colleges to institutionally facilitate civic engagement; but students' ethical development within those experiences can occur with intentionality or by happenstance.

To most effectively educate students for PSR, practitioners must intentionally structure civic engagement initiatives as parts of a metacurricular intervention designed to produce the intended learning outcomes, reflecting theoretically sound practices. University context, relational aspects, and opportunities for student and academic affairs collaboration influence the design of PSR-focused civic engagement strategies. Organizational support and incentives, campus culture and environments, and appropriate faculty and staff support are needed to effectively promote and assess these initiatives. Currently, only a few campuses have "thought through an overall framework for civic and political education that is comprehensive, coherent, conceptually clear, and developmentally appropriate" (Carnegie Foundation for the Advancement of Teaching, 2006, p. 3), much less civic engagement activities for the development of PSR—but colleges now can and should do so.

References

Adams-Gaston, J., Jacoby, B., and Peres, P. "Creating an Institutional Culture to Advance Civic Engagement and Leadership," April 15, 2005. Retrieved December 23, 2011, from http://www.aacu.org/meetings/pdfs/POE05Jacoby.pdf.

NEW DIRECTIONS FOR STUDENT SERVICES • DOI: 10.1002/ss

Association of American Colleges and Universities. *Core Commitments: Educating Students for Personal and Social Responsibility* [Brochure]. Washington, D.C.: Association of American Colleges and Universities, n.d.

Association of American Colleges and Universities. "Leading Researchers Explore How to Measure the Impact of College on Personal and Social Responsibility" [Press release]. May 14, 2004. Retrieved September 16, 2007, from http://www.aacu.org/press_room/press_releases/2004/Templeton.cfm.

Association of American Colleges and Universities. "AAC&U Announces National Initiative on Fostering Personal and Social Responsibility in Today's College Students." 2006. Retrieved March 22, 2009, from http://www.aacu.org/press_room/press_releases/2006/CoreCommitmentsInitiative.cfm.

Association of American Colleges and Universities. *College Learning for the New Global Century* [Report]. Washington, D.C.: Association of American Colleges and Universities, 2007.

Banning, J. (ed.). *Campus Ecology: A Perspective for Student Affairs: A NASPA Monograph.* Cincinnati: National Student Personnel Association, 1978.

Bickel, R. D., & Lake, P. F. (1999). *The Rights and Responsibilities of the Modern University: Who Assumes the Risks of College Life?* Durham, N.C.: Carolina Academic Press.

Boyd, K. D. "The Nature of the Student-Institution Relationship and Behavioral Indicators of Personal and Social Responsibility: An Exploration of the Association Between Relational Quality Outcomes, Alcohol Use and Academic Honesty." Unpublished doctoral dissertation. Retrieved from Proquest, 2010.

Boyd, K. D., and Cooper, D. L. "Embracing the Student–Institution Relationship: Creating a Connection Conducive to Personal and Social Responsibility." Paper presented at the annual conference of the Association for the Study of Higher Education, Jacksonville, Fl., 2008.

Boyte, H., and Hollander, E. "Wingspread Declaration on Renewing the Civic Mission of the American Research University." 1999. Retrieved December 23, 2011, from http://www.compact.org/wp-content/uploads/2009/04/wingspread_declaration.pdf.

Carnegie Foundation for the Advancement of Teaching. *Campus Life: In Search of Community.* Princeton, N.J.: Carnegie Foundation for the Advancement of Teaching, 1990.

Carnegie Foundation for the Advancement of Teaching and the Center for Information and Research on Civic Learning and Engagement. "Higher Education: Civic Mission & Civic Effects." Stanford, Calif.: Carnegie Foundation for the Advancement of Teaching, 2006. Retrieved December 23, 2011, from http://www.carnegiefoundation.org/sites/default/files/publications/elibrary_pdf_633.pdf

Chickering, A. *Maximizing Civic Learning and Social Responsibility.* ASHE Reader. Reprinted from *New England Resource Center for Higher Education*, Printed Monograph/Paper-Boston, MA, New England Resource Center for Higher Education, 2001,463–467.

Colby, A., Beaumont, E., Ehrlich, T., and Corngold, J. *Educating for Democracy: Preparing Undergraduates for Responsible Political Engagement.* Stanford, Calif.: Jossey-Bass, 2007.

Colby, A., Ehrlich, T., Beaumont, E., and Stephens, J. "Undergraduate Education and the Development of Moral and Civic Responsibility." Education Position Papers, the Communitarian Network, n.d. Retrieved December 23, 2011, from http://www.gwu.edu/~ccps/papers_reports_education.html.

Colby, A., Ehrlich, T., Beaumont, E., and Stephens, J. *Educating Citizens: Preparing America's Undergraduates for Lives of Moral and Civic Responsibility.* San Francisco: Jossey-Bass, 2003.

Colby, A., and Sullivan, W. M. "Strengthening the Foundations of Students' Excellence, Integrity, and Social Contributions." *Liberal Education*, 2009, 95(1), 22–29.

Ehrlich, T. (ed.). *Civic Responsibility and Higher Education.* Phoenix, Ariz.: American Council on Education and Onyx Press, 2000.

Foubert, J. D., and Newberry, J. T. "Effects of Two Versions of an Empathy-Based Rape Prevention Program on Fraternity Men's Survivor Empathy, Attitudes, and Behavioral Intent to Commit Rape or Sexual Assault." *Journal of College Student Development*, 2006, 47, 133–148.

Hersh, R. H., and Schneider, C. G. "Fostering Personal & Social Responsibility on College & University Campuses." *Liberal Education*, 2005, 91(3), 6–13.

Jacoby, B. *Civic Engagement in Higher Education*. San Francisco: Jossey-Bass, 2009.

Kohlberg, L. *The Philosophy of Moral Development: Essays on Moral Development* (Vol. 1). San Francisco: Harper & Row, 1981.

Kohlberg, L. *The Psychology of Moral Development: Essays on Moral Development* (Vol. 2). San Francisco: Harper & Row, 1984.

Kuh, G. D., Kinzie, J., Schuh, J. H., Whitt, E. J., and Associates. *Student Success in College*. San Francisco: Jossey-Bass, 2005.

Libbey, H. P. "Measuring Student Relationships to School: Attachment, Bonding, Connectedness, and Engagement." *Journal of School Health*, 2004, 74, 274–283.

Loukas, A., Suzuki, R., and Horton, K. D. "Examining School Connectedness as a Mediator of School Climate Effects." *Journal of Research on Adolescence*, 2006, 16, 491–502.

McCabe, D. L. "It Takes a Village: Academic Dishonesty." *Liberal Education*, 2005, 91(3), 26–31.

McCabe, D. L., and Trevino, L. K. "Academic Dishonesty: Honor Codes and Other Contextual Influences." *Journal of Higher Education*, 1993, 64, 522–538.

McCabe, D. L., and Trevino, L. K. "What We Know About Cheating in College: Longitudinal Trends and Recent Developments." *Change*, 1996, 28(1), 28–33.

McCabe, D. L., Trevino, L. K., and Butterfield, K. D. "Academic Integrity in Honor Code and Non-Honor Code Environments: A Qualitative Investigation." *The Journal of Higher Education*, 1999, 70, 211–234.

Miller, T. E., Bender, B. E., Schuh, J. H., and Associates. *Promoting Reasonable Expectations: Aligning Student and Institutional Views of the College Experience*. San Francisco: Jossey-Bass, 2005.

Musil, C. M. "Educating Students for Personal and Social Responsibility: The Civic Learning Spiral." In B. Jacoby and Associates, *Civic Engagement in Higher Education: Concepts and Practices*. San Francisco: Jossey-Bass, 2009.

Nassi, A. J. "Survivors of the Sixties: Comparative Psychosocial and Political Development of Former Berkeley Student Activists." *American Psychologist*, 1981, 36(7), 753–761.

Newman, F. *Higher Education and the American Resurgence*. Stanford, Calif.: Carnegie Foundation for the Advancement of Teaching, 1985.

Pace, C. R., & Stern, G. "An Approach to the Measurement of Psychological Characteristics of College Environments." *Journal of Educational Psychology*, 1958, 49, 269–277.

Pascarella, E. T., and Terenzini, P. T. *How College Affects Students: A Third Decade of Research*. San Francisco: Jossey-Bass, 2005.

Perry, W. G. *Forms of Ethical and Intellectual Development in the College Years: A Scheme*. San Francisco: Jossey-Bass, 1999.

Rest, J., Narvaez, D., Bebeau, M. J., and Thoma, S. J. *Postconventional Moral Thinking: A Neo-Kohlbergian Approach*. Mahwah, N.J.: Lawrence Erlbaum, 1999.

Rosas, M. "College Student Activism: An Exploration of Learning Outcomes." Unpublished doctoral dissertation, University of Iowa, 2010.

Rudolph, F. *The American College and University: A History*. Athens: University of Georgia Press, 1962.

Saltmarsh, J. "The Civic Promise of Service Learning." *Liberal Education*, 2005, 91(2), 50–55.

Sprinthall, N. A., and Scott, D. "Promoting Psychological Development, Math Achievement, and Success Attribution of Female Students Through Deliberative Psychological Education." *Journal of Counseling Psychology*, 1989, 36(4), 440–446.

Strange, C. C., and Banning, J. H. *Educating by Design: Creating Campus Learning Environments That Work.* San Francisco: Jossey-Bass, 2001.

Swaner, L. E. "Educating for Personal and Social Responsibility: A Planning Project of the Association of American Colleges and Universities." 2004. Retrieved November 27, 2011, from http://www.aacu.org/core_commitments/documents/review_of_lit_000.pdf.

Swaner, L. E. "Educating for Personal & Social Responsibility: A Review of the Literature." *Liberal Education*, 2005, 91(3), 14–21.

KAREN D. BOYD *is a visiting instructor at the University of Central Florida.*

SARAH BRACKMANN *is a doctoral candidate in the Institute of Higher Education at the University of Georgia.*

NEW DIRECTIONS FOR STUDENT SERVICES • DOI: 10.1002/ss

5

This chapter describes the history of conduct and moral learning in higher education and offers suggestions for future conduct practice.

Conduct Systems Designed to Promote Moral Learning

James M. Lancaster

Historically, those responsible for administration of student conduct resolution in U.S. higher education have sought some manner of moral development for students, whether labeled as such or not. It is clear that contemporary conduct officers are more deeply concerned with such student development as an extension of their practice. Many such professionals may frame the question as "What am I trying to accomplish with this student, and why?" In this chapter, I explore the history of student conduct systems; discuss the evolution of learning, development, and conduct; and consider the conduct professional as moral mentor.

History of Student Conduct Systems

Rudolph (1991), in his classic history of American higher education, noted that early colonial colleges were religiously affiliated, offering concern for morality focused through the lens of a traditional, narrow religious belief system. As the influence of religious affiliation diminished and more secular institutions emerged, the president of the institution, or sometimes faculty and, still later, the individual who would come to be known as the dean usually were charged with managing student behavior and conduct and shaping that conduct around some version of the moral values of their society.

Even when not expressly stated, student conduct and moral development as a part of learning were implied and entwined themes throughout early higher education in this country. From the early twentieth century until the 1960s, the Supreme Court decision in *Gott v. Berea* (1913) defined the view that "college authorities stood *in loco parentis* concerning the

NEW DIRECTIONS FOR STUDENT SERVICES, no. 139, Fall 2012 © Wiley Periodicals, Inc.
Published online in Wiley Online Library (wileyonlinelibrary.com) • DOI: 10.1002/ss.20022

physical and moral welfare and mental training of the pupils" (Kaplin and Lee, 1997, p. 6). Although this decision had the unfortunate effect of defining college students as minor children, it had the salutary aspect of embedding the concept of moral training in college, albeit from a parental perspective.

In a more substantive statement addressing the role of moral development specifically within the emerging student affairs profession, the *Student Personnel Point of View* (discussed in Chapter One) provided one of the earliest and clearest statements of the administrator's historic and continuing concern with moral development of college students: "This philosophy imposes upon educational institutions the obligation to consider the student as a whole—his intellectual capacity and achievement, his emotional make up, his physical condition, his social relationships, his vocational aptitudes and skills, his moral and religious values" (American Council on Education, 1937, p. 3). This concern was echoed in the 1949 edition of this document as well.

As student development and moral education continued to evolve, the 1961 case of *Dixon v. Alabama* produced a decision changing higher education law and the practice of conduct administrators. While litigated under Fourteenth Amendment constitutional issues, the case modeled essential moral and ethical development dilemmas for students and universities. Arising from the 1960s activist culture in which students in Alabama and elsewhere found themselves, the *Dixon* case initiated case law that marked a change in the relationship between students and their educational institutions, signaling the end of *in loco parentis*. *Dixon* heralded a turn toward due process in conduct proceedings and, while not clearly required by this or subsequent cases, the beginnings of a more structured and legalistic practice of student conduct. Yet a close reading of the *Dixon* case finds ethical and moral concepts, such as fair or fairness, scattered throughout the decision.

The presenting issues in *Dixon* were about moral and ethical decision making. The actions of the student defendants charged in the *Dixon* case were clearly those of moral principle even if viewed through the lens of political–legal–social opportunity issues that also drove the case. The students' response to segregation suggested moral sensitivity, judgment, motivation, and actions, all elements of what, in hindsight, we can see Rest (1986) subsequently describing as the four components of moral development.

The recognition of student rights in *Dixon* empowered students to think about the consequences and implications of their actions in a manner that reflected ethical questions. Administrators, in turn, had cause to reflect on how their institutions would react to a student body that could no longer be dismissed as children. Could rule making and enforcement coexist with educational goals based in holistic and moral development? Did students experience learning in activities and institutional processes beyond the formal classroom? The exploration and resolution of these issues informed textbooks, teaching, and practice concerns in student conduct practices that persist to the present.

Learning, Development, and Conduct

Theories of moral development, based in part on the works of Kohlberg, Gilligan, Rest, and others, had appeared in the late 1950s and early 1960s. In particular, James Rest's *Theory of Moral Development* (1986) began to influence the conversation about approaches to contemporary conduct processes. Responding to theorists as well as the evolving debates about how students learn, the leading student development professional associations, the American College Personnel Association (ACPA) and the National Association of Student Personnel Administrators (NASPA), provided forums and position papers in which the place of moral development was a continuing theme. In 1996, ACPA issued a document titled *Principles of Good Practice for Student Affairs* and later joined NASPA in commissioning *Professional Competency Areas for Student Affairs Practitioners* (2010). Both documents emphasized the important role that student affairs professionals played in pursuing learning outcomes that assist students in the development of values, ethical standards, and ethical decision-making practices— all factors in creating an environment of moral community and development for college students. Conduct administrators from every era of education have come to agree that such complex issues involving moral and ethical dilemmas, rather than simple questions of right and wrong, have been at the heart of many of their most serious conduct cases. In recent years, student conduct professionals and researchers have advocated a role for conduct administration in facilitating the development of appropriate moral sensibilities in their work with students (Taylor and Varner, 2009).

The Association for Student Judicial Affairs (ASJA), a new professional association for conduct officers founded in 1986, implied in its name a bias for "judicial affairs." But early ASJA documents stated, "The membership of ASJA believes that a primary purpose for the enforcement of such standards is to maintain and strengthen the ethical climate and to promote the academic integrity of our institutions" (1964). The name of the organization was eventually changed to the Association for Student Conduct Resolution, intended to better reflect the growing awareness of and emphasis on conduct resolution, in all of its forms, rather than the suggestive legalistic approach of "Student Judicial Affairs" (Association for Student Conduct Administration, 2011). A review of annual conference proceedings from 1996 to the present reflects this growing interest and orientation toward programs answering ethical and moral development concerns among members (Association for Student Conduct Administration, 1996–2010).

NEW DIRECTIONS FOR STUDENT SERVICES • DOI: 10.1002/ss

Student Conduct Outcomes as Moral Learning

By the early 1990s, questions of philosophy, learning, and their place in the practice of student conduct created a dialogue about the necessity for more intentional consideration of ethical and moral development in the conduct process. David Hoekema, in 1994's *Campus Rules and Moral Community*, concluded that "[m]orality on campus ... is formed and shaped in dialogue.... We are moral beings because we are beings who live in community and who shape our ideals in dialogue" (p. 164). Writing in 1997, Dannells suggested that the process of conduct should be based on a clear recognition and conveyance of institutional–community values. Citing Chickering and Reisser's 1993 work in *Education and Identity*, Dannells also affirmed the role that conduct systems could play in facilitating moral learning and development.

Strike and Moss (1997) expressed the need for new ways of approaching decision making and, by extension, student conduct, describing the essential nature of a campus "as a kind of moral community" (p. 2). Cooper and Lancaster (1998) presented a succession of articles on this theme and concluded that institutions, rather than only seeking risk reduction and policy explication, must define their moral and ethical expectations for student conduct processes.

Bickel and Lake (1999) called the old model of university relations with students (including conduct processes) legalistic, proposing instead that administrators act as facilitators or as "a guide who provides as much support, information, interaction, and control as is reasonably necessary and appropriate in the situation" (p. 193). Although not speaking specifically of student conduct or of moral development per se, the authors could certainly be perceived as developmental.

Lancaster (2003) offered a summative argument for reflective practices emphasizing an "intentional practice," synthesizing ethical and legal concerns into a holistic focus on student conduct resolution. Editors of the 2008 edition of *The Complete Guide to Student Conduct Practice* encouraged a holistic philosophy of practice in student conduct, answering the structural, legal needs of the practice while recognizing and encouraging the "reasoned, thoughtful, and developmental" aspects of practice (Lancaster and Waryold, p. 293).

The result of this dialogue is a contemporary professional practice of student conduct that reflects a variety of procedural options. Schrage and Thompson (2009) described these options as a "spectrum" of practice wherein a thoughtful conduct professional demonstrates the "ethic of justice and care" in the choice of a resolution procedure appropriate to the legal and ethical needs of the participants while also attending to students' holistic development. These processes, ranging from very informal to highly structured formal procedures, included the options of dialogue, conflict coaching, facilitated dialogue, mediation, restorative practices

NEW DIRECTIONS FOR STUDENT SERVICES • DOI: 10.1002/ss

(including restorative justice), shuttle diplomacy, informal adjudication, and formal adjudication through hearings.

In this space it is impractical to fully discuss the details of each of these approaches. But the editors' and author's intent is clear: They seek to unite the various forms of conduct resolution that have emerged over the last few years into a common spectrum of options. From this approach, the average conduct professional may gain a clearer insight about available options and thus examine more deeply the particular needs of each student situation related to conduct as well as likely developmental and moral learning outcomes. It is significant that dialogue is a stated component in many of these options. Dialogue provides an opportunity for ethical inquiry with students concerning the intent and actual meaning of the actions that led to their present involvement with a conduct office.

In theory, a broad array of options for resolution of conduct issues, especially as they encourage dialogue, offers powerful tools for those who seek to be moral mentors. Wise and thoughtful choices among such options can suggest to students the professional's commitment to the welfare of the participants; it may also offer an opportunity for students to see the potential to resolve differences in a humane and developmentally appropriate manner, perhaps different from the less thoughtful choices that resulted in the need for conduct proceedings. Successful mastery of such a broad and complex array of resolution options requires a professional who is knowledgeable of the options, responsive to the needs of each student, and experienced in conduct practices. A professional practice of this subtlety demonstrates a commitment on the part of the professional that is the consummate moral response to the challenges of student learning in conduct settings.

Himbeault and Varner (2009) affirm the power of these alternative forms of dispute resolution. They contend that "what is lacking in [the historical] risk-reduction model is [this] conscious decision to support individual growth in the areas of moral and ethical decision making, social identity development, cultural competency, and other components of psychosocial development theory" (p. 23).

The Conduct Professional as Moral Mentor

A common thread of concern for moral development has now been woven into of the tapestry of conduct resolution options. The choices in processes available to professional conduct officers allow them great freedom in choosing how to move students to renewed sensitivity about ethics, judgment, and the moral basis of their actions. This set of outcomes can be viewed as one desirable definition of success in contemporary student conduct resolution. But even the most impressive array of tools from which to choose does not alone define a successful professional or ensure moral mentoring. Relationships, and the quality of those relationships, between conduct officers and students also matter deeply. Experienced conduct officers affirm this whenever they gather for discussions at conferences. How one models moral mentoring is potentially as critical to professional success as any array of process tools.

Recent research by Stimpson and Janosik (2011) documents the impact of this relationship in conduct settings. In a broad survey of approximately 4,000 students at twenty-three different institutions, they found that student learning in conduct processes is directly and strongly correlated with the student perception that the process was a fair one. The perception of fairness can exist only when the professional relationship with the student ensures it.

Fairness, as suggested by Kitchener (1985), is a derivative of the core ethical principles of being just and being faithful, something that has been cited as central to human relationships. It is reasonable to suggest that building a relationship that explores the moral concerns of conduct rather than a simple recitation of rules and regulations and findings of right and wrong conveys such qualities much more successfully. There is broad consensus about the value of educational and moral development and the importance of building relationships that model as well as prescribe right or, we might suggest, moral behavior. Experienced conduct officers today would likely agree that a positive relationship with student conduct participants, modeling ethical principles and moral conduct, has always been important in creating a perception that such behavior is not only desirable and preferable but also offers student conduct participants a pathway to success in their campus community and in their subsequent lives.

In such relationships, the authenticity of the moral mentor, or what Palmer (2004) terms the wholeness of a life that affirms rather than denies one's selfhood, is critical. As moral mentors, we must be who we say we are. For example, we cannot suggest moderation in consumption of alcohol to a student accused of alcohol abuse and then model such excess and misbehavior in our own lives. Such an approach is not only lacking in authenticity; it is corrosive to the very idea of moral mentoring. The student's perception of duplicity in the behavior of this professional not only damages the mentoring relationship; it calls into question the entire notion of moral models. We therefore undertake moral mentoring with regard for our own actions and intents as well as with due respect for the fragility of the relationship we seek to nurture.

How, then, might a newly appointed student conduct officer approach the creation and implementation of a conduct system designed to promote moral learning?

James Rest's Four Component Model (1986) offers a framework for guidance.

Moral Sensitivity. Conduct processes are based on the institutional code of conduct in which the philosophy of moral development must be clearly defined in all resolution options. If members of a university community who participate in and for whom conduct professionals facilitate meaning perceive this exercise of moral development options, they will become powerful allies in this process. By providing this foundation, first through training and then by accurately modeling these concepts throughout all resolution processes, the conduct professional demonstrates *moral sensitivity* in philosophy and in practice.

But, in acknowledging that one type of resolution process does not fit all situations, the professional must be well informed about the many resolution possibilities, adept in their employment, equipped to assess both moral and developmental learning outcomes in their practice, and prepared to alter processes as the situation demands. To take our earlier example of a student abusing alcohol, certainly a common misconduct on college campuses, moral sensitivity by the conduct officer might reflect the acknowledgment that every such case is different and that, in some cases, very different processes and outcomes might be necessary and appropriate to create learning outcomes useful to the student and appropriate to the concerns of a campus community's restorative and social justice concerns.

Moral Judgment. Selection of the appropriate process, or course of action for the conduct case, must balance institutional and student interests in an ethically correct manner, rejecting distracting or merely expedient lines of thinking in favor of those based on moral principles. Exercising *moral judgment* requires the professional to constantly assess this balance, giving close attention to the specifics of the situation as well as the fairest manner for resolution while acknowledging any inherent shadows or biases he or she may possess. Student participants, through appropriate facilitation with a professional, perceive the reason for the choice of particular forms of resolution as well as their meaning and will benefit directly from this aspect of moral mentoring. Continuing the alcohol abuse scenario, a conduct officer whose childhood was dominated by an alcoholic parent is called on to acknowledge this bias, work hard against it in choosing and assessing resolution options, and, in some situations, perhaps recusing him- or herself from the case.

Moral Motivation. Once the resolution possibilities are reviewed and the appropriate process selected, the professional commits to the chosen course of action, keeping in mind the moral values inherent in this resolution choice while acknowledging other conflicting values or concerns. Students involved in these choices within the framework of the conduct process begin to understand the moral component of the professional's work. The display of this *moral motivation* is the beginning of the persistence necessary for a successful resolution of the conflict, reflecting sensitivity, awareness, and judgment as well as motivation. Both the professional and the student participants will gain insight into the moral underpinnings of the process and the commitment of the professional to moral development.

NEW DIRECTIONS FOR STUDENT SERVICES • DOI: 10.1002/ss

The student accused of abusing alcohol might activate the professional's deeply held religious or personal belief that drinking is "wrong." Yet when the accused student is properly assigned to a full conduct board hearing, the most stringent of processes, it is not because the conduct officer is motivated to punish the student harshly but because the officer recognizes that the hearing procedure offers the broadest opportunity for the student to fairly be heard and understood by an impartial and representative panel.

Moral Action. Perhaps the most difficult step in conduct resolution can be the moment of decision in the case. At this stage, it is critical that the professional demonstrate the courage to act with integrity, acknowledging what has already been determined as the appropriate process and conscious of the principles and moral values involved in the decision. This demonstration of *moral action* is often most difficult specifically because it involves a final commitment to moral rather than emotional, political, or other competing concerns. It may also be an inherently risky stage for the professional as it may compete directly with concerns of other affected students as well as various stakeholders, including supervisors, families, or other community members. All participants, and especially those who are termed victims in the process, must have clarity about what the process is designed to accomplish and, as important, what the process may not provide.

Moral action can provide a powerful voice for victims, but such outcomes often can be perceived only in the longer term, thus providing little immediate satisfaction. Even when not immediately accepted by all stakeholders, conduct resolution that intentionally seeks moral development and learning, when properly conceived, provides the foundation for extended moral learning for all participants. The alcohol-abusing student is found "responsible," and the penalty recommended is suspension. The conduct officer as a student experienced mercy in a similar situation and is loath to treat the student more harshly than he himself was treated. Yet a course of moral action trusts in the integrity of the panel's judgment, acknowledges the fairness of a sanction well within prescribed boundaries, and affirms the recommendation despite personal feelings.

Institutional Support

Student conduct professionals do not exercise their responsibilities in isolation of a theoretical model. There are many constituents necessarily considered and involved in the construction of a moral development conduct process. Support of the institutional community is also vital to success. Sanctions must reflect the intended learning outcomes of the process. Administrative superiors have an important role to play in supporting the development and application of the philosophy and moral development aspects that will be included in the conduct code as the foundation for the professional's work.

NEW DIRECTIONS FOR STUDENT SERVICES • DOI: 10.1002/ss

A professional practice based in moral learning and development that has meaning for the student(s) and institution, consistently seeks to reflect these attributes in all parts of the process, and is clarified constantly through meaning-making activities for students facilitated by the conduct professional as well as more formal assessment activities. The practice of the conduct moral mentor begins with the commitment to a wide array of conduct process possibilities and extends through the initial resolution process for each case and beyond. Frequently, meaning making in the moral development process evolves over time as individuals come to reflect on and understand the deeper aspects of their experiences.

The perception of fairness serves as the basis for a relationship between professional and student from which future learning can emerge. Employing a theoretical model of moral development can activate submerged moral values of the participants. The combination of a distinctive environment conducive to the conveyance of these values and the creation of expectations, appropriate processes, and procedures (with time allocated for necessary reflection and meaning making), successful and consistent moral learning outcomes may be achieved. In all of this, the commitment to moral action and learning as a philosophy must be clearly conveyed by the professional's actions and in a manner accessible to and appropriate for students' developmental level. The professional must highlight and reinforce moments in which the student demonstrates any level of response to the moral concerns inherent in this practice.

Final Thoughts for Practice. The resolution of student conduct today is pursued through a variety of processes, each of which can reflect moral mentoring intentions. Although there are clear legal boundaries and directives as well as institutional policies that the professional must consider, all of the available processes discussed in this chapter may meet these requirements while functioning within a philosophy of moral mentoring. No single process can be said innately to stand alone on the moral high ground; each has value in certain situations. There are no guarantees of success in the efforts of a conduct moral mentor. But it is important to acknowledge that any process will be less successful and potentially harmful without a skilled professional who, acknowledging all of the contextual requirements of conduct resolution, intentionally attempts the facilitation of moral learning outcomes. The conduct professional's actions in every process are a singular and vital element in delivering on the promise of moral mentoring. The emotional intelligence, informed intuition, and moral clarity of the conduct professional, in addition to the areas of practical knowledge and process, are critical to a desired outcome of moral development for the student. The careful cultivation, selection, and pursuit of a moral development intent and philosophy in conduct processes by a student conduct professional will result not only in resolution of the events at hand; it also will provide opportunities for moral growth and development for the student and the community.

References

American Council on Education. "The Student Personnel Point of View," 1937, 1 (3). *American Council of Education Studies.* Retrieved December 10, 2011, from http://www.myacpa.org/pub/documents/1937.pdf.

American College Personnel Association. Principles of Good Practice For Student Affairs, 1996. Retrieved December 10, 2011, from http://acpa.nche.edu/pgp/principle.htm.

American College Personnel Association and the National Association of Student Personnel Administrators. *Professional Competency Areas for Student Affairs Practitioners,* 2010. Retrieved December 2, 2011, from http://www.naspa.org/programs/profdev/default.cfm.

Association for Student Conduct Administration, "History of ASCA," 2010. Retrieved August 2, 2011, from http://www.theasca.org/history/.

Association for Student Conduct Administration, *Conference Proceedings.* College Station, Texas: Association for Student Conduct Administration], 1996–2010.

Association for Student Judicial Affairs. *Statement of Ethical Principles and Standards of Conduct.* College Station, Texas: Association for Student Judicial Affairs, 1964.

Association for Student Judicial Affairs. "Ethical Principles and Standards of Conduct," 1993. Retrieved August 2, 2011, from http://www.theasca.org/ethicalprinciples/.

Bickel, R. D., and Lake, P. F. *The Rights and Responsibilities of the Modern University: Who Assumes the Risks of College Life.* Durham, N.C.: Carolina Academic Press, 1999.

Chickering, A., and Reisser, L. *Education and Identity,* 2nd ed. San Francisco: Jossey-Bass, 1993.

Cooper, D., and Lancaster, J. (eds.). *Beyond Law and Policy: Reaffirming The Role of Student Affairs.* New Directions for Student Services, no. 82. San Francisco: Jossey-Bass, 1998.

Dannells, M. *From Discipline to Development: Rethinking Student Conduct in Higher Education.* ASHE-ERIC Higher Education Report 25, No. 2. Washington, D.C.: George Washington University Graduate School of Education and Human Development, 1997.

Dixon v. Alabama, 294 F. 2d 150 (5th Cir. 1961).

Gott v. Berea College, et al., 156 Ky. 376; 161 S.W. 204; 1913 Ky. LEXIS 441 (1913)

Himbeault, S. T., and Varner, D. T. "When Student Learning and Law Merge to Create Educational Student Conflict Resolution and Effective Conduct Management Programs." In. J. M. Schrage and N. G. Giacomini, *Reframing Campus Conflict: Student Conduct Practice Through a Social Justice Lens.* Sterling, VA: Stylus Publishing, 2009.

Hoekema, D. *Campus Rules and Moral Community: In Place of In Loco Parentis.* Lanham, Md.: Rowman & Littlefield, 1994.

Kaplin, W., and Lee, B. *A Legal Guide for Student Affairs Professionals.* San Francisco: Jossey-Bass, 1997.

Kitchener, K. "Ethical Principles and Ethical Decisions in Student Affairs." In H. J. Cannon and R. D. Brown (eds.), *Applied Ethics in Student Services.* New Directions for Student Services, no. 30. San Francisco: Jossey-Bass, 1985.

Lancaster, J. (ed.) *Exercising Power with Wisdom: Bridging Legal and Ethical Practice with Intention.* Asheville, N.C.: College Administration Publications, 2003.

Lancaster, J., and Waryold, D. (eds.). *Student Conduct Practice: The Complete Guide for Student Affairs Professionals.* Sterling, Va.: Stylus, 2008.

Palmer, P. *A Hidden Wholeness: The Journey Toward an Undivided Life.* San Francisco: Jossey-Bass, 2004.

Rest, J. *Moral Development: Advances in Research and Theory.* Westport, Conn.: Praeger, 1986.

Rudolph, F. *The American College and University: A History*. Athens: University of Georgia Press, 1991.

Schrage, J., and Thompson, M. "Providing a Spectrum of Resolution Options." In J. Schrage and N. Geist Giacomini (eds.), *Reframing Campus Conflict: Student Conduct Practice Through a Social Justice Lens*. Sterling, Va.: Stylus, 2009.

Stimpson, M. T., and Janosik, S. M. "The Conduct System and Its Influence on Student Learning." Manuscript, 2011.

Strike, K., and Moss, P. *Ethics and College Student Life*. Needham Heights, Mass.: Allyn & Bacon, 1997.

Taylor, S. H., and Varner, D. T. "When Student Learning and Law Merge to Create Educational Student Conflict Resolution and Effective Conduct Management Programs." In J. Schrage and N. Geist Giacomini (eds.), *Reframing Campus Conflict: Student Conduct Practice Through a Social Justice Lens*. Sterling, Va.: Stylus, 2009.

JAMES M. LANCASTER is a professor of human development and psychological counseling at Appalachian State University.

NEW DIRECTIONS FOR STUDENT SERVICES • DOI: 10.1002/ss

6

This chapter considers the role of pluralism and social justice education in promoting moral growth among college students using Rest's Four Component Model. Implications of these issues and recommendations for the promotion of moral maturity for social justice action are offered.

Promoting Moral Growth Through Pluralism and Social Justice Education

Dafina Lazarus Stewart

Issues of morality, including deciding among competing values and negotiating obligations to self and community, are pervasive and saturate many aspects of life. This chapter explores the role of educating for pluralism and social justice in promoting moral growth among college students. Rest's four-component model of moral maturity (reviewed by Liddell and Cooper in Chapter One) frames this discussion. The chapter concludes with implications and recommendations for the design and implementation of intentional diversity and social justice experiences.

Framing the Conversation

There are several approaches to the exploration of diversity, inclusion, and social justice in higher education contexts. These approaches include different philosophical orientations (Manning, 2009), communication strategies (Nash, 2010), and the ways that different language signals philosophical orientation and mission (Shuford, 2011). This chapter grounds itself in a philosophical orientation that integrates multicultural competence and social justice (Reason and Watson, 2011), meaning that it takes an affective, cognitive, and skills-based approach to addressing issues of power, privilege, and equity. Moreover, in this chapter, I use the term "pluralism" instead of "diversity" or "multiculturalism" and focus on "social justice" instead of focusing only on empathy, civility, and tolerance.

Pluralism. The understanding of pluralism that grounds this discussion is informed by a definition of community that sees differences as valuable and educationally purposeful (Palmer, 1993a). As such, I understand pluralism to include not only the robust presence of diversity but also the

NEW DIRECTIONS FOR STUDENT SERVICES, no. 139, Fall 2012 © Wiley Periodicals, Inc.
Published online in Wiley Online Library (wileyonlinelibrary.com) • DOI: 10.1002/ss.20023

engagement with diversity that seeks to build trust and rapport across lines of difference as a multicultural skill (Pope, Reynolds, and Mueller, 2004). In this view, pluralism does not seek to assimilate diversity into a preexisting homogeneous community but rather allows diversity to shape and transform an ever-evolving community of engaged heterogeneity. In this way, engaging pluralism shifts diversity from being a mere fact of life to a complex process of recognizing, responding to, and negotiating the differences in power that diversity embodies in systems characterized by oppression (Mueller and Broido, 2012).

Social Justice. The absence of empathy, civility, and tolerance reflects a lack of moral maturity and undermines the development of pluralistic communities in higher education. Yet limiting the discussion to only those elements fails to seek social justice as an outcome for diverse, pluralistic communities. Social justice, as Bell (2007) discussed, "is both a process and a goal" that seeks the "full and equal participation of all groups in a society that is mutually shaped to meet their needs" (p. 1). Social justice also embraces processes that are "democratic and participatory" (p. 2) and grounded in affirming human agency to work collaboratively toward change.

Pluralism and Social Justice in Higher Education

For as long as colleges and universities have existed in the United States, issues of diversity and multiculturalism have intersected with discussions regarding access, equality, and inclusion. As reviewed by Mueller and Broido (2012) and summarized by Kupo (2011), higher education has slowly transformed from a social system marked exclusively for white, wealthy, young men. Legal challenges and policy reversals have led to the expansion of access to higher education. Through this advocacy work, progress has been made, albeit unevenly, toward the redress of racial, ethnic, sex, and ability barriers. Although advocacy continues on these issues, current efforts seek to acknowledge and transform structures of inequality related to religion, gender identity and expression, sexual orientation, economics, and age as well. In order to move college and university environments from communities merely characterized by diversity to those marked by inclusive engagement, multicultural competence and social justice pedagogy must become familiar tools for campus professionals. These are discussed further next.

Multicultural Competence. Campus professionals are called on to demonstrate multicultural competence to effectively address the growing diversity of college and university campuses and nurture the development of pluralistic campus communities. The ability to effectively respond to and address issues of equity and inclusion has been recognized as a core competency for student affairs educators (Pope, Reynolds, and Mueller, 2004; American College Personnel Association and National Association of

Student Personnel Administrators, 2010). Multicultural competence incorporates the awareness, knowledge, and skills needed to work in culturally diverse environments in meaningful, productive, and effective ways. Moreover, multicultural competence is useful in building relationships across lines of difference and to make effective interventions in support of social justice in colleges and universities (Pope, Reynolds, and Mueller, 2004). In this context, multicultural competence extends beyond race and ethnicity to any issue where differences of identity, beliefs, and experiences are shaped by societal systems of power and privilege.

Multicultural competence has three dimensions: multicultural awareness, multicultural knowledge, and multicultural skills (Pope, Reynolds, and Mueller, 2004). Multicultural awareness, the affective dimension, involves continuing self-evaluation, correction of false assumptions and information, and developing a personal commitment to social justice and change. Multicultural knowledge, focused on cognitive complexity, includes having extensive and accurate content knowledge about various populations as well as how systems of privilege and oppression impact people's experiences on campus. Multicultural skills, the behavioral dimension, include effective communication, gaining trust, exercising appropriate challenge and support, and the ability to make culturally sensitive and appropriate interventions. Creating campus environments that embrace and nurture pluralism requires the practice of multicultural competence.

Social Justice Education. Social justice seeks full democratic and participatory engagement of individuals to create anti-oppressive systems, structures, and communities. As a theoretical framework, social justice incorporates a theory of oppression, characterized as pervasive, restrictive, hierarchical, internalized, and involving relationships that are complex, multiple, and cross-cutting (Bell, 2007). Further, a theory of oppression sees the shared and distinctive patterns of various systems of domination. Social justice seeks change processes that utilize collaborative relationships between members of dominant and subordinated groups. The objectives and learning outcomes of social justice education are to equip learners with the tools needed to initiate and sustain transformation for pluralism in their communities, including the campus. The development of agency to feel capable and responsible for helping to create change is also a desired outcome and may complement Rest's (1986) discussion of courage and motivation.

To create socially just environments that are culturally responsive and pluralistic, campus professionals must use multicultural competence to frame discussions that challenge and revise institutional systems of privilege and oppression through reimagining policies, seeking affirmative representation, and dismantling networks of privilege. Facilitating growth in moral maturity is an effective means for helping learners engage issues of pluralism and social justice.

Applying Rest's Model to Pluralism and Social Justice Education

James Rest's (1986) model of moral maturity (discussed more extensively in Chapter One) creates a useful frame to explore applications related to pluralism and social justice. Specific activities and experiences that can encourage learners to mature in each component are recommended. Examples are provided to demonstrate how each component may relate to issues of pluralism and social justice.

Moral Sensitivity. Moral sensitivity requires individuals to interpret a situation as one that involves moral issues. Being sensitive to moral issues means being able to identify the ways in which decisions, policies, relationships, and structures may involve the need to negotiate commitments to self and others. In a social justice framework, being morally sensitive means being alert and attentive to how systems and structures unevenly distribute power, resources, and opportunity and issues of collusion and internalized dominance and oppression.

For example, a unit supervisor has been directed to build more collaboration and morale among the staff in the unit. Does requiring participation in evening team-building activities unevenly burden staff members with caregiver responsibilities? How might common meals and potlucks demonstrate religious privilege by not taking dietary restrictions into account or economic privilege by assuming that everyone can afford to purchase extra food? There are many ways to build morale and collaborative relationships, but moral sensitivity is needed to discern which ideas will lead to socially just outcomes and which will not.

Moral Judgment. Moral judgment is about reasoning through the complexity of the cognitive structures employed to make decisions about how one should act (Rest, 1986). Issues of pluralism and social justice involve moral judgment by provoking deliberations about intervening to change policies and structures. Moral judgment is required when deciding what constitutes "right action" in our personal relationships with others. Is it right, fair, or socially just to treat people or groups uniquely, or should we seek to treat all groups the same? The level of complexity required to answer this question is related to multicultural knowledge regarding the reality of unequal distributions of power, status, resources, opportunity, and dignity.

Exercising moral judgment means going beyond asking the questions posed in the example regarding how to promote staff collaboration and morale. It also invites the consideration of what principles best help to rectify the conflicts among meeting others' needs equitably in this situation. Advanced moral judgment takes into consideration self, others, and community as moral equals (Gilligan, 1994/1977) to decenter normative ways of being and doing that lead to privilege and oppression.

Moral Motivation. Moral motivation involves making decisions about why one should act on moral judgments from the previous component (Rest, 1986). Ultimately, moral motivation requires sifting through competing priorities and choosing to elevate moral values above one's self-interest. In the language of multicultural competence, moral motivation is most deeply connected to multicultural awareness as it requires not only valuing diversity but also internalizing the will to commit oneself to social justice action.

Moral motivation, and by extension multicultural awareness, can be facilitated through any activity that challenges people to clarify and sort through their values and possible courses of action (Dalton, 1985). For example, it would be helpful for the unit supervisor to discuss the issue with the staff directly as well as with a trusted colleague. Moral motivation illustrates the importance of community and relationship to moral action. Community and relationships are also critical to effective social justice advocacy.

Moral Character. The final component in Rest's (1986) model is moral character—or putting one's values into action to behave in morally defensible ways. Issues of moral character involve understanding the consequences of moral action and an examination of the barriers that prevent one from taking action. In a social justice framework, moral character development promotes taking "paths of least resistance" (Johnson, 2006, p. 80) to ruthlessly examine one's privilege and take responsibility for deliberate, intentional, sustained action on behalf of the fair and equitable distribution of resources. Strong moral character also leads individuals to seek out engagement in pluralistic communities and to work to create pluralism where it does not yet exist.

Actualizing moral character requires identifying and dismantling the barriers (such as fears) that prevent action. By preparing for resistance, people may be better equipped to take persistent action necessary for long-term, sustainable change to occur. Campus professionals should also be prepared to encounter resistance from others as they begin to realize the costs of moral action (Dalton, 1985). Activities that focus on multicultural skill development, summarized earlier, can lead to the strengthening of moral character. In the example of the unit supervisor, this professional should be prepared to justify the chosen course of action and find allies and sources of support for promoting socially just outcomes.

Reflection. The example used here may not have contained an obvious social justice issue. Indeed, it is rarely the obvious issues of justice and fairness that individuals struggle with. Instead, more challenging are the subtle ways that innocuous situations, such as attempting to promote better staff collaboration and morale, can undermine best intentions regarding pluralism and social justice. In actual practice, applying Rest's (1986) model requires having reflective conversations that demonstrate the multicultural skills described by Pope, Reynolds, and Mueller (2004). These conversations must take place before, during, and after moral decisions. Social justice advocacy is most effective when the contexts of relationships among people living and working together in community are considered. This includes attending to issues of building trust and rapport across lines of difference, the willingness to admit errors, and knowing how to intervene to prevent oppressive outcomes.

Implications and Recommendations

Student affairs educators have a vital role to play in supporting moral growth through affirming pluralism and social justice education. Some suggestions for developing a pedagogy of social justice education, as well as strategies for handling resistance, are presented next.

Pedagogy of Social Justice Education. Effective social justice pedagogy requires considering the *process* of learning as well as its *content.* Adams (2007) identified five frameworks for social justice education that may be relevant in promoting moral growth. First, educators should tend to both the affective and cognitive aspects of learning. Palmer (1993b) also asserted the importance of creating a space for emotions as a legitimate aspect of the learning process. Discussions of values, beliefs, and behaviors can agitate emotional responses. Understanding *how* learners feel about moral issues involved in pluralism and social justice is intimately connected to what learners *think* about these issues. For instance, economic insecurity and high anxiety about being able to provide for one's family may be connected to opposition to immigration reform or admitting undocumented students to study at U.S. colleges and universities. Such feelings can also be used as a gateway to empathy and from there to more cognitively complex understandings of immigration patterns and the experiences of undocumented immigrants in the United States.

Second, Adams (2007) advocated for educators to acknowledge individual experiences as well as social group patterns. Members of privileged social groups may have difficulty acknowledging social group memberships, while those in subordinated groups may prioritize those group memberships. It is important for members in both privileged and subordinated groups to value the ways that the complexities of identities in oppressive frameworks distinguish individual experiences among members of the same social group, as well as the commonalities shared by social group members (Strange and Stewart, 2011).

A third issue to consider is how power and privilege influence the mentoring relationship due to differences in professional status, race, gender, or other social hierarchies (Adams, 2007). Student affairs professionals must be careful not to exercise "power over" others to promote moral maturity but rather "power with" (Bell, 2007, p. 2) to collaboratively work toward greater moral maturity. Ignoring the ways in which professionals, usually unconsciously, can reinforce oppressive power dynamics can undermine the relationship and jeopardize the development of moral maturity.

NEW DIRECTIONS FOR STUDENT SERVICES • DOI: 10.1002/ss

Considering how to effectively use reflection and experience to promote learning is fourth (Adams, 2007). This advice affirms the cycle of active learning espoused by David Kolb (1984) that situated the incorporation of new learning in providing space for reflection both individually and with others, as well as opportunities for practice. Strategies for processing dissonance-generating experiences are explored in more detail in Chapter Two.

The final core framework in the pedagogy of social justice education outlined by Adams (2007) is to acknowledge and reward progress. Change is risky and will not be attempted without clear and explicit support. It is essential that campus professionals also assume the role of encourager and champion for others as they develop moral maturity.

Engaging Resistance. Conversations about pluralism and social justice will likely turn into what Watt (2007a) calls *difficult dialogues*. Watt defined a difficult dialogue as "a verbal or written exchange of ideas or opinions between citizens within a community that centers on an awakening of potentially conflicting views of beliefs or values about social justice issues" (p. 112). When participants are engaged in a difficult dialogue, typically they are confronted with their own privileges and differing opinions about equity and one's responsibility to correct injustice. These conflicts trigger normal human reactions arising from either fear or a sense of entitlement that Watt (2007b) described in the Privileged Identity Exploration (PIE) model. As individuals learn new information about themselves or others, they are prompted to recognize and contemplate their privileged identities and then consider how and whether to take action based on this new awareness that is anchored in social justice (Watt, 2007b).

When people first recognize their privileged identity, *denial, deflection,* and *rationalization* may characterize their initial responses (Watt, 2007b). These defenses deny the roots of internalized dominance and cultural hegemony that may be contributing to their decision making. Such excuses may also deflect responsibility for enacting social justice in the campus environment to others or blame oppression on structural issues that people feel powerless to address. Finally, these defenses can rationalize injustice to be the natural outcome of demographics, instead of the result of the intentional exclusion and forced assimilation of minority voices in a diverse society. Such defenses may be commonly used in discussions about improving recruitment and retention of a diverse student body or in how to represent diversity in campus marketing materials. Resistance on the grounds of presumed value differences between groups, complaints about the lack of diversity in the college's surrounding community, or defending exclusive representations by appealing to majority interests all reflect these defenses in operation.

The next level of responding to one's privilege, contemplating privilege, may provoke different defenses, particularly what Watt (2007b) labeled *intellectualization, principium,* and *false envy.* These defenses refuse to acknowledge and respect the ways in which social group memberships may shape and inform individual identity and meaning making. Such defenses also treat one's own belief systems as superior to others and as the final criteria for determining just action regardless of how others are affected. Finally, although seemingly harmless, the self-deprecation used in false envy fails to appreciate the complex issues of exclusion, dominance, and cultural appropriation that can be created when unity is defined as conformity. These defenses may come out in several ways on campus. For example, employing religious dogma to challenge expanding benefits and services to the lesbian, gay, bisexual, transgender, and queer community on campus reflects principium. Providing only support for cultural performances without opportunities for members of those groups to engage in critiques of institutional policies and systems is a manifestation of false envy.

Addressing privileged identities is the third category of defenses in Watt's (2007a, 2007b) model and includes *benevolence* and *minimization.* These defenses fail to challenge systems of injustice. For example, although campus canned food drives may be beneficial, advocating for changes in the systems that lead to the need for food pantries goes beyond benevolence to actual social justice transformation. Additionally, the process of creating a pluralistic and socially just community is reduced to a checklist one can review or a one-time training session. Socially just residence hall environments, for example, are not created simply by having residence hall staff attend a diversity training workshop at the beginning of the year. Instead, multiple training sessions throughout the year, both proactive and reactive, continual reflective conversations, and consistent leadership are necessary. Thinking one can engender pluralism and social justice by just knowing what mistakes to avoid misses the point of what it means to seek full and equitable participation and sharing of resources in a democratic society.

Summary. It is a difficult and complex process to raise critical consciousness and demonstrate multicultural competence (Johnson, 2006; Adams, 2007; Watt, 2007b). There is no final destination in the development of critical consciousness. Student affairs professionals must remain attentive to their own learning and development regarding pluralism and social justice. Resistance can be anticipated, prepared for, and effectively refuted. The challenge of demonstrating multicultural competence does not have to prevent the development of moral maturity. Rather, engaging in difficult dialogues and practicing patience, compassion, and forgiveness assist with the continual development of moral maturity. Student affairs professionals can be effective mentors and colearners by acknowledging the fatigue felt by engaging in this process and genuinely caring about those under their charge (Baxter Magolda, 2001; Watt, 2007b).

NEW DIRECTIONS FOR STUDENT SERVICES • DOI: 10.1002/ss

Conclusion

Issues of achieving pluralism and social justice in our relationships, communities, and society are moral issues that can benefit from an intentional, developmental approach to facilitating moral maturity. As guides and co-learners, student affairs professionals can help to promote moral maturity by recognizing the morality of pluralism and social justice. Doing so will transform colleges and universities for the better.

References

Adams, M. "Pedagogical Frameworks for Social Justice Education." In M. Adams, L. A. Bell, and P. Griffin (eds.), *Teaching for Diversity and Social Justice*, 2nd ed. New York: Routledge, 2007.

American College Personnel Association and National Association of Student Personnel Administrators. *Professional Competency Areas for Student Affairs Practitioners*, 2010. Washington, D.C.: American College Personnel Association and National Association of Student Personnel Administrators. Retrieved June 20, 2012, from http://www2. myacpa.org/au/governance/Joint_Task_Force_of_Professional_Competencies.php

Baxter Magolda, M. B. *Making Their Own Way: Narratives for Transforming Higher Education to Promote Self-Development*. Sterling, Va.: Stylus, 2001.

Bell, L. A. "Theoretical Foundations for Social Justice Education." In M. Adams, L. A. Bell, and P. Griffin (eds.), *Teaching for Diversity and Social Justice*, 2nd ed. New York: Routledge, 2007.

Dalton, J. *Promoting Values Development in College Students*. Monograph Series, Vol. 4, National Association of Student Personnel Administrators, 1985.

Gilligan, C. "In a Different Voice: Women's Conceptions of Self and of Morality." In B. Puka (ed.), *Caring Voices and Women's Moral Frames: Gilligan's View* (Vol. 6, pp. 1–37). New York: Garland Press, 1994. (Reprinted from *Harvard Educational Review*, 1977, 47[4], 481–517.)

Johnson, A. G. *Privilege, Power, and Difference*, 2nd ed. Boston: McGraw-Hill, 2006.

Kolb, D. A. *Experiential Learning: Experience As the Source of Learning and Development*. Upper Saddle River, N.J.: Prentice-Hall, 1984.

Kupo, V. L. "Remembering Our Past to Shape Our Future." In D. L. Stewart (ed.), *Multicultural Student Services On Campus: Building Bridges, Re-visioning Community*. Sterling, Va.: Stylus, 2011.

Manning, K. "Philosophical Underpinnings of Student Affairs Work on Difference." *About Campus*, 2009, *14*(2), 11–17. doi:10.1002/abc.284

Mueller, J., and Broido, E. M. "Historical Context: Who We Were is Part of Who We Are." In J. Arminio, V. Torres, and R. L. Pope (eds.), *Are we there yet? Taking personal responsibility for creating an inclusive campus* (pp. 57–101). Sterling, VA: Stylus, 2012.

Nash, R. J. "What Is the Best Way to Be a Social Justice Advocate? Communication Strategies for Effective Social Justice Advocacy." *About Campus*, 2010, *15*(2), 11–18. doi:10.1002/abc.20017

Palmer, P. J. "Community, Conflict, and Ways of knowing," 1993a. Center for Courage and Renewal. Retrieved December 10, 2011, from http://www.couragerenewal.org/parker/writings/community-conflict.

Palmer, P. J. *To Know as We are Known: Education as a Spiritual Journey*. San Francisco: HarperCollins, 1993b.

Pope, R. L., Reynolds, A. L., and Mueller, J. A. *Multicultural Competence in Student Affairs*. San Francisco: Jossey-Bass, 2004.

Reason, R., and Watson, K. "Multicultural Competence and Social Justice Advocacy." In
    D. L. Stewart (ed.), *Multicultural Student Services on Campus: Building Bridges,
    Re-visioning Community*. Sterling, Va.: Stylus, 2011.
Rest, J. *Moral Development: Advances in Research and Theory*. New York: Praeger, 1986.
Shuford, B. C. "Historical and Philosophical Development of Multicultural Student Ser-
    vices." In D. L. Stewart (ed.), *Multicultural Student Services on Campus: Building
    Bridges, Re-visioning Community*. Sterling, Va.: Stylus, 2011.
Strange, C. C., and Stewart, D. L. "Preparing Diversity Change Leaders." In D. L.
    Stewart (ed.), *Multicultural Student Services on Campus: Building Bridges, Re-visioning
    Community*. Sterling, Va.: Stylus, 2011.
Watt, S. K. "Editor's Notes." *College Student Affairs Journal*, 2007a, 26(2), 112–113.
Watt, S. K. "Difficult Dialogues, Privilege and Social Justice: Uses of the Privileged Iden-
    tity Exploration (PIE) Model in Student Affairs Practice." *College Student Affairs Jour-
    nal*, 2007b, 26(2), 114–126.

*DAFINA LAZARUS STEWART is an associate professor of higher education and
student affairs at Bowling Green State University.*

NEW DIRECTIONS FOR STUDENT SERVICES • DOI: 10.1002/ss

7

This chapter operationalizes "sustainability" using the triple bottom line of environmental, social, and economic sustainability as well as ways moral action is inherently present in a variety of sustainability practices

Sustainability as Moral Action

Merrily S. Dunn, Jeanne S. Hart-Steffes

The concepts and dilemmas that draw us into conversations about moral action are complex, multidimensional, and, at the same time, as simple as the Golden Rule: Treat others as you would like to be treated. When we consider sustainability as a moral action, there are equally complex realities at hand—climate change, resource depletion, water and land rights. One author describes this broad sense of sustainability as "the connection of specific social and environmental problems to the functioning of human and ecological systems" (Jenkins, 2011, p. 97). Yet one of the most commonly accepted definitions of sustainability argues simply that it is "the ability to meet the needs of the current generation without compromising the ability of future generations to meet their needs" (World Commission on Environment and Development, 1987, p. 8).

The focus of the conversation on sustainability as moral action is situated in a higher education and student affairs context and encourages action through the broad application of ideas and resources for social change. This expanded definition of sustainability includes a holistic integration of social and economic equity along with an environmental focus. Edwards (2005) wrote that this expanded definition "requires a systems perspective focused on relationships among numerous stakeholders" (p. 29). It is within the context of a connected set of relationships and thinking about "the other–each other" that the full notion of sustainability as moral action can be and will be realized.

Higher education, in its role as creator and disseminator of knowledge, will help solve social problems (poverty, illiteracy, homelessness) and advance/enhance life skills (arts, literature, teaching). Education is a significant medium through which the population can gain access, equity, and opportunity. If we consider education the great equalizer (Mann, 1848), enabling us to solve problems and ensure the survival of our world, a

NEW DIRECTIONS FOR STUDENT SERVICES, no. 139, Fall 2012 © Wiley Periodicals, Inc.
Published online in Wiley Online Library (wileyonlinelibrary.com) • DOI: 10.1002/ss.20024

sustainability model inclusive of environmental, social, and economic aspects will move us in that direction. This broader, more inclusive representation of sustainability is defined as the triple bottom line (Elkington, 1997). Sustainability, articulated through moral action, leads to social change and ultimately social justice. When we act sustainably, our actions lead us to think holistically about our world and all those in it; we act in a socially just way so that all of humanity can reach their full potential.

Traditional definitions and tasks focused on sustainability limited the discussions to environmental sustainability. The more contemporary working definition for sustainability is better explained through the combination of environment and social and economic aspects, or the triple bottom line (Elkington, 1997). Timpson and others (2006) state that the community efforts of the triple bottom line "become especially important as we pushed past individual disciplinary silos and focused sustainability as a reflection of environmental, economic, and societal factors" (p. xvi). They continue: "[A] more holistic, interconnected perspective makes sense in both practical and theoretical terms. Complex topics resist simplistic, reductionistic analyses and, instead, require sophisticated interdisciplinary thinking and creativity. And so it is with the study of sustainability" (p. xvi). When considering sustainability within a holistic, interconnected context, it can parallel Rest's (1986) Four Component Model of Moral Development. Both models, the triple bottom line and Rest's, define and, in some ways, require a connected, holistic journey.

Sustainability as an Act of Social Justice

This connection is evident on closer inspection of Rest's model. As referenced to in Chapter One, James Rest's research on moral reasoning outlined four components necessary for such reasoning to occur. Rest begins with moral sensitivity, alertness for a need for a particular activity, often in response to cues from the environment (Rest, Narvaez, Bebeau, and Thoma, 1999). A student is aware that his or her community is in an extreme drought and thinks about the length of a typical shower, multiplied by 600 students living in a residence hall, or that same community letting the water run while brushing their teeth. Once this moral sensitivity or awareness is present, Rest's second component, moral judgment, is engaged to determine which course of action is right or fair (Rest, 1986). Our drought-aware student wonders if talking to the residence hall staff about putting controls on the showers that limit the amount of water each student could use would be effective or if talking to the residence hall government about a campaign to educate students about water usage and impact might be more effective. Third, the commitment a person makes to a course of action defines moral motivation (Rest, 1986). Engaging the residence hall government becomes the choice for this student, who decides that having stu-

NEW DIRECTIONS FOR STUDENT SERVICES • DOI: 10.1002/ss

dents take part in decision making rather than imposing restrictions on them is the better course of action. Finally, moral action is having the character to take the determined course of action (Rest, 1986). The student designs a plan of education and related programming, with input from the student government. Having moved through Rest's model, the student offers to head up these efforts to help the community become more sustainable.

From Individual Moral Action to Intentional Social Change

Institutional mission statements call us to educate for citizenry, both global and local. In our role as educators, supporting and challenging students to use greater sophistication in moral reasoning becomes a component of educating for social change. A strong mechanism aiding us in this work is the Social Change Model of Leadership Development, created by the Higher Education Research Institute (Komives and Wagner, 2009). The model's focus is on students working together, with each in a leadership role, seeking to understand the multitude of perspectives around a wide array of social problems present in our quickly changing, increasingly global world. The model is built on seven values interacting around and through change. The values are divided naturally into those related to the group (collaboration, common purpose, controversy with civility), the individual (consciousness of self, congruence, commitment), and the larger society–community (citizenship) (Komives and Wagner, 2009). This model serves two important functions in working with students around issues of sustainability as we frame this for them as moral action grounded in moral reasoning. First, as illustrated previously, Rest's model provides a map for students thinking about issues of sustainability—just as it does for other issues of social justice, such as poverty, homelessness, racism, and sexism. The Social Change Model assists students in operationalizing their thinking by giving them a structure on which to hang the different aspects of what they think. Returning to our student in the drought—her moral awareness is consciousness of self when thinking about the role she plays in the drought every time she takes a shower or brushes her teeth. She comes to this level of knowledge only by understanding her own values—a process engaged in her arrival at moral sensitivity. Once she has arrived at her decision to volunteer to lead the sustainability efforts in the face of the drought, she has embraced the role of change—the ultimate goal being improving the status quo. The student made the individual sacrifice for the greater good. Her willingness to put the needs of many ahead of her own self-interest is what makes this an inherently moral question. She has moved through moral judgment, making decisions congruent with her values in order to make the moral commitment that leads to moral action. Once she is engaged in the change process with the residence hall student government, the Social

Change Model emphasizes group values that put the good of the larger society as the ultimate goal, the ultimate good. This model provides students a structure that illuminates their work for social change and, ultimately, social justice (Komives and Wagner, 2009).

Sustainability as Spirituality

The example of student commitment to sustainability as outlined by the previous example shows the connection through the lens of the Social Change Model (Komives and Wagner, 2009) with the logical connections to Rest's model (1986). This example highlights just one of many ways that our connection to the earth and advocating on its behalf can be conceptualized as social justice and moral action. Another is the concept of stewardship, used in multiple contexts: religious, fiscal, and environmental. Its use relative to the management of natural resources has become commonplace and is defined similarly to the definition of sustainability used earlier in this chapter. A hallmark of the definition is the attention paid to current and future generations, other species, and private as well as common good (Worrell and Appleby, 2000).

One facet of sustainability sometimes forgotten in our construction of it as a social issue is its necessary grounding in science and growth from natural resource management, ecology, and environmental science (Worrell and Appleby, 2000; Carroll, 2004). Scholars in religion, spirituality, and philosophy discuss the relationship between sustainability and religion (Bauman, Bohannon, and O'Brien, 2011) and reason and faith as dance partners in the spirituality of sustainability (Carroll, 2004). Ultimately, though, the conversation between science and spiritual or religious aspects of sustainability comes down to a question of choice. How do we choose to interact with nature (Evanoff, 2011)? For many, these choices about our relationship to the natural world, our stewardship of it, and our commitment to sustainability are choices both spiritual and moral. The application of Rest's model of moral decision making, with its components of sensitivity, judgment, motivation, and action, reflects those thought patterns, leading to action, exhibited by students who ground their commitment to sustainability as an exercise of their faith or as an expression of their spirituality lived in their daily lives. Examples can be as extensive as the student who starts a new student organization committed to educating the campus community about the role each member plays in creating a sustainable environment or as simple as the student choosing to bike to campus rather than drive. They are as diverse as the faculty member who includes the location of recycling containers as part of an orientation to the class environment and the college president who includes a commitment to sustainability as part of the annual state of the university address. The audiences, the impact, and the scope vary, but the intent of each includes a commitment to the future through an act of sustainability.

NEW DIRECTIONS FOR STUDENT SERVICES • DOI: 10.1002/ss

Sustainability in a Student Affairs Context

The formal introduction of sustainability to student affairs is recent at the professional association level. The emergence of student affairs practitioners and scholars into the arena of sustainability has been quickly followed by guidelines regarding professional training and development (Kerr and Hart-Steffes, 2012). In 2006, the American College Personnel Association (ACPA) Sustainability Taskforce was established. Similar work is also under way in a number of student affairs and related professional associations, such as the Association of College and University Housing Officers-International (ACUHO-I) with extensive resources related to sustainability; the National Association of Student Personnel Administrators (NASPA) with a sustainability knowledge community; and the Association for the Advancement of Sustainability in Higher Education (AASHE).

When the ACPA Sustainability Taskforce convened, one of its first tasks was the creation of a set of sustainability student learning outcomes. The student learning outcomes presented in *Learning Reconsidered* (American College Personnel Association and National Association of Student Personnel Administrators, 2004) were used as a model. Several student learning outcomes for sustainability parallel Rest's model, including:

- Understanding the definition of sustainability
- Relating values and how those values impact others (moral sensitivity, judgment)
- Using knowledge to change behavior (moral motivation, judgment)
- Change agent skill acquisition and application in the larger world context (moral judgment, action, and reasoning) (Rest, Narvaez, Bebeau, and Thoma, 1999)

There are many tangible ways in which college students engage in moral action while participating in sustainability activities. Some of the most common include service-learning and civic engagement projects (Checkoway, 2011). It can be argued that through such activities, colleges and universities exercise their commitment to the overarching goal of educating students for a life of service and active citizenship (Colby, Ehrlich, Beaumont, and Stephens, 2003). Additionally, sustainability activities provide another example of how moral action is manifested as social justice in ways understood through the social change model. Students come together around issues related to sustainability, allowing them to collaborate around a shared purpose with the ultimate goal of bringing positive change on behalf of and in their environment (Komives and Wagner, 2009). Students, in the United States and globally, have been resourceful in creating opportunities to live out their expressed values and improve the social condition of others and their environments. Historically, many colleges and universities have had service as a focus of their work, their values, and their missions guiding educational practice (Kenney, Dumont, and Kenney, 2005). Examples of private institutions where students have focused on sustainability as part of their service mission include Tufts University, Furman University, and Harvard University.

An example of how students have incorporated service and civic engagement into their college experience include the "Ten Tons of Love" program, a year-end recycle reuse program coordinated by Syracuse University. Last year forty-five "tons of love" were donated to local charities. Another example is "The One Thing Challenge," a sustainability-focused competition between the University of Washington and Washington State.

Many institutions coordinate alternative spring break programs that sponsor service trips in the United States and worldwide. A number of institutions find creative ways to keep sustainability at the center of their mission of educating for social justice through such programs. Duke University offers students the opportunity to participate in the local food movement in their community. North Carolina State students learn about rain forest conservation in Costa Rica. The Jewish Renaissance Project at Penn State provides students the chance to work on an organic California farm active in community-supported agriculture. These programs are examples of how institutions of higher education have embraced sustainability and social justice as a vehicle to help develop and enhance thinking and doing for "the other," resulting in students' greater stewardship of resources.

Sustainability at an Institutional Level as Moral Action

Several national programs have encouraged the development of sustainability on college campuses. The largest and most well-known is the American College and University Presidents' Climate Commitment (ACUPCC). The ACUPCC:

> Is a high-visibility effort to address global climate disruption ... to eliminate net greenhouse gas emissions from specified campus operations, and to promote the research and educational efforts of higher education to equip society to re-stabilize the earth's climate. Its mission is to ... educate students, create solutions, and provide leadership-by-example for the rest of society [www.presidentsclimatecommitment.org, 2007].

As of September 2011, there were approximately 700 signatories of the ACUPCC. Efforts to integrate sustainability into the fabric of the campus have been growing as well. Although this is arguably positive progress, it also raises questions regarding the role of institutional finance and politics as potential barriers to greater participation in organizations such as ACUPCC and more extensive and systemic commitments to sustainability.

NEW DIRECTIONS FOR STUDENT SERVICES • DOI: 10.1002/ss

The integration of sustainability in higher education and student affairs has positive effects throughout the enterprise (Kerr and Hart-Steffes, 2012). The use of local contractors, goods, and tradespeople has connected the campus with the local community in specific and much-needed ways, generating local job growth. These community connections have added significant resources to local economies. The holistic approach necessitates the community as part of the campus culture; the reuse, reduce, and recycle process saves money and better utilizes resources. Many institutions have marketed and promoted "Being Green" as a significant selling point for their current and prospective students as well as alumnae. Surveys from the *Princeton Review* have shown that a substantial number of prospective students find this an important attribute when selecting colleges (Kerr and Hart-Steffes, 2012). The use of renewal energy can have a significant effect in lowering costs and making smaller footprints (Putman and Philips, 2006). These examples are crucial in furthering issues of sustainability, but the argument can be made that higher education has not been transformed by the imperatives of sustainability in ways that many theorists believe it must be in order for the necessary outcomes to be realized (Wals and Blewitt, 2010).

Assessing Sustainability

Assessment of programs and learning is important to all higher education professionals (Bresciani, 2006). Integrating a culture of assessment in student affairs is crucial to establish evidence and provide credibility for our work in general (Sandeen and Barr, 2006; Schuh and Associates, 2009; Seagraves and Dean, 2010) and specifically related to sustainability (Kerr and Hart-Steffes, 2012). The best-known and largest assessment tool for sustainability that has been used by student affairs professionals is the Sustainability Tracking Assessment and Rating System (STARS). STARS is a transparent, self-reporting framework for colleges and universities to gauge relative progress toward sustainability. STARS was developed by the Association for the Advancement of Sustainability in Higher Education (AASHE) with broad participation from the higher education community.

STARS is a ranking system, *not* a rating system; it is designed as a guide to help advance and develop the entire campus enterprise. This ranking system is structured so that an institution conducts a self-guided (unless otherwise designed) inventory to assess their level of involvement in three main categories: Education and Research; Operations; and Planning, Administration, and Engagement. Even if an institution does not assess all three areas, the tool is a valuable guide to understand and consider aspirational goals and levels of excellence when beginning or continuing the sustainability conversation on campus (Kerr and Hart-Steffes, 2012).

Campuses can also track their sustainability efforts in their investments and endowments. Socially responsible investing allows colleges and universities to use a social screen to choose their investment portfolio. These investments seek to maximize financial good and social good. Socially responsible investing includes those companies that promote diversity, the environment, fair labor standards, and human and consumer rights, and that avoid alcohol, gambling, weapons, pornography, and tobacco. The governing boards of the two largest professional student affairs organizations, ACPA and NASPA, have policies for socially responsible investing (Kerr and Hart-Steffes, 2012).

Resources to help institutions as they work to greater effectiveness in issues of sustainability including a primer on sustainability, learning outcomes, program ideas, and tool kits can be found at www.myacpa.org/task%2Dforce/sustainability/. Other professional associations previously mentioned—NASPA, ACUHO-I, and AASHE—also provide significant assistance to institutions and the practitioners working in them around specific sustainability questions. Numerous references used in the writing of this chapter are also instructive. *Sustainability on Campus*, edited by Barlett and Chase (2004), is particularly thorough and insightful.

Although the utility and importance of these resources should be obvious, it is also crucial to understand and face the challenges and barriers inherent in working for sustainability on college campuses. Barlett and Chase (2004) note that rather than considering sustainability a problem to be solved, it should be thought of as a vision of what our future can be, complete with a "map" that will allow us to find our way. The map must be coupled with a conversation about purpose and goals. Why is it important to educate each other for and about a sustainable future? What are the moral, philosophical, and societal issues that assist or prevent us from seeking answers to allow us to find our way? Two goals might be to raise sensitivity and understanding and to encourage individuals and institutions toward action.

Institutions of higher education can be significant catalysts and serve as champions and role models for a more sustainable future. Examples of sustainable policies and practices that many campuses have included in their map include:

- Electric and hybrid cars in a motor pool
- Discounted public transportation coupons or tickets
- Highly desirable or discounted parking spaces for vehicles used to carpool
- Weekly "meatless Friday" or "local Mondays" to reduce the food print of dining services
- On-campus farmers' markets featuring local produce
- Food rescue programs in the dining halls (which would support food banks and community shelters)
- Online course management tools
- Bicycle lending pools

These are just a few ways in which institutions have embraced sustainability and served as role models for their communities. In each of these situations, there may have been a single person or a small group of committed campus members who had a goal of making their campus a better global steward. Their individual and collective actions can be explained and in some ways understood utilizing the sustainability learning outcomes and Rest's Four Component Model of Moral Development (1986) and the Social Change Model (Komives and Wagner, 2009).

References

American College and University Presidents' Climate Commitment. "Mission and History," 2007. Retrieved June 20, 2012, from http://www.presidentsclimatecommitment. org/about/mission-history.

American College Personnel Association. *Toward a Sustainable Future: The Role of Student Affairs in Creating Healthy Environments, Social Justice, and Strong Economies.* Washington, D.C.: American College Personnel Association, 2008.

American College Personnel Association and National Association of Student Personnel Administrators. *Learning Reconsidered: A Campus-Wide Focus on the Student Experience.* Washington D.C.: American College Personnel Association and National Association of Student Personnel Administrators, 2004. Retrieved from www.myacpa.org/pub/documents/learningreconsidered.pdf.

Barlett, P. F., and Chase, G. W. (eds.). *Sustainability on Campus: Stories and Strategies for Change.* Cambridge, Mass.: MIT Press, 2004.

Bauman, W. A., Bohannon, R. R. II, and O'Brien, K. J. (eds.). *Grounding Religion: A Field Guide to the Study of Religion and Ecology.* New York: Routledge, 2011.

Bresciani, M. J. *Outcomes-Based Academic and Co-Curricular Program Review: A Compilation of Institutional Good Practices.* Sterling, Va.: Stylus, 2006.

Carroll, J. E. *Sustainability and Spirituality.* Albany: State University of New York Press, 2004.

Checkoway, B. "New Perspectives on Civic Engagement and Psychosocial Well Being." *Liberal Education*, 2011, 97(2), 6–11.

Colby, A., Ehrlich, T., Beaumont, E. and Stephens, J. *Educating Citizens: Preparing America's Undergraduates for Lives of Moral and Civic Responsibility.* San Francisco: Jossey-Bass, 2003.

Edwards, A. R. *The Sustainability Revolution: Portrait of a Paradigm Shift.* Gabriolo Island, B.C.: New Society, 2005.

Elkington, J. *Cannibals with Forks: The Triple Bottom Line of 21st Century Business.* Oxford: Capstone, 1997.

Evanoff, R. *Bioregionalism and Global Ethics: A Transactional Approach to Achieving Ecological Sustainability, Social Justice, and Human Well-being.* New York: Routledge, 2011.

Jenkins, W. "Sustainability." In W. A. Bauman, R. R. Bohannon II, and K. J. O'Brien (eds.), *Grounding Religion: A Field Guide to the Study of Religion and Ecology.* New York: Routledge, 2011.

Kenney, D. R., Dumont, R., and Kenney, G. S. *Mission and Place: Strengthening Learning and Community Through Campus Design.* Westport, Conn.: Praeger, 2005.

Kerr, K., and Hart-Steffes, J. S. "Sustainability, Student Affairs, and Students." *New Directions in Student Services*, 2012, (137), 7–17.

Komives, S. R., and Wagner, W. E. *Leadership for a Better World: Understanding the Social Change Model of Leadership Development.* San Francisco: Jossey-Bass, 2009.

Mann, H. "Horace Mann on Education and National Welfare: Twelfth Annual Report of Horace Mann as secretary of Massachusetts State Board of Education," 1848. Retrieved November 26, 2011, from http://www.tncrimlaw.com/civil_bible/horace_mann.htm.

Putman, A., and Phillips, M. *The Business Case for Renewable Energy: A Guide for Colleges and Universities.* Washington, D.C.: APPA, National Association of College and University Business Officers, and Society for College and University Planning, 2006.

Rest, J. *Moral Development: Advances in Research and Theory.* New York: Praeger, 1986.

Rest, J., Narvaez, D., Bebeau, M. and Thoma, S. *Postconventional Moral Thinking: A Neo-Kohlbergian Approach.* Mahwah, N.J.: Lawrence Erlbaum, 1999.

Sandeen, A., and Barr, M. J. *Critical Issues for Student Affairs: Challenges and Opportunities.* San Francisco: Jossey-Bass, 2006.

Schuh, J., and Associates. *Assessment Methods for Student Affairs.* San Francisco: Jossey-Bass, 2009.

Seagraves, B., and Dean, L. A. "Conditions Supporting a Culture of Assessment in Student Affairs Divisions at Small Colleges and Universities." *Journal of Student Affairs Research and Practice,* 2010, 47(3), 307–324.

Timpson, W. M., Dunbar, B., Kimmel, G., Bruyere, B., Newman, P. and Mizia, H. *147 Practical Tips for Teaching Sustainability.* Madison, Wisc.: Atwood, 2006.

Wals, A. E. J., and Blewitt, J. "Third Wave Sustainability in Higher Education: Some (inter)national Trends and Developments." In P. Jones, D. Selby, and S. Sterling (eds.), *Sustainability Education: Perspectives and Practice across Higher Education* (pp. 55–74). London, UK: Earthscan, 2010.

World Commission on Environment and Development. *Our Common World. Oxford.* Oxford: Oxford University Press, 1987.

Worrell, R., and Appleby, M. C. "Stewardship of Natural Resources: Definition, Ethical and Practical Aspects." *Journal of Agricultural and Environmental Ethics,* 2000, 12, 263–277.

MERRILY S. DUNN is an associate professor at the University of Georgia.

JEANNE S. HART-STEFFES is the vice president for student affairs and dean of students at Western New England College.

NEW DIRECTIONS FOR STUDENT SERVICES • DOI: 10.1002/ss

8

How can we help students and mentees aspire to be their best? Doing so does not require perfection, but it does call on us to help students engage with their imperfections while owning our own.

The Role of the Campus Professional as a Moral Mentor

Margaret A. Healy, James M. Lancaster, Debora L. Liddell, Dafina Lazarus Stewart

As student affairs professionals, we traditionally struggle with how to bring the proper balance to our work. Our critics and we often frame this as a question of holistic practice in which we attempt to balance the educational with the recreational and the developmental with the authoritarian. These critics often focus on how issues of moral development during the college years are addressed by student development professionals, especially with regard to the spiritual and value-based frames that may arrive with students from home, religious, and social environments (National Association of Scholars, 2008). Our anxiety as student affairs professionals about our role in moral development arises in part from those critics who assert that our work is simply to reinforce classroom instruction and avoid any efforts that might be labeled moral development. Yet our students want and need this mentoring.

College students' search for meaning and purpose is widely documented (Astin, Astin, and Lindholm, 2010), and campus professionals are well situated to help them find it.

Our work takes place in a variety of settings—some informal, some structured. In each of these settings, we may find opportunity to serve as moral mentors. James Rest (1986), in his description of the four components of moral development, begins with the need for what he terms "moral sensitivity." A starting point for the practice of moral mentoring involves the realization that the diversity of our practice settings should provoke us to be particularly aware of the need for our own moral sensitivity. From wherever we presume to undertake this work, it is critical that we be clear about the meaning of the term "moral mentor," for both our own purposes

NEW DIRECTIONS FOR STUDENT SERVICES, no. 139, Fall 2012 © Wiley Periodicals, Inc.
Published online in Wiley Online Library (wileyonlinelibrary.com) • DOI: 10.1002/ss.20025

and to forestall a debate on irrelevant semantics both within and external to our profession. For the purposes of this discussion, we describe the moral mentor as a professional practicing in the field of student affairs, concerned holistically with student development, of which a significant part is moral development. This professional works within the framework discussed in Chapter One of this volume, as one who is focused on moral development as an aspect of cognitive development, assisting students in meaning making and decision making, where moral actions are weighed and moral principles serve as the boundaries for those actions.

Our framework for such work is grounded in theory, experience, and professional standards including, among others, the Professional Competency Areas for Student Affairs Practitioners (American College Personnel Association and National Association of Student Personnel Administrators, 2010) and the Council for the Advancement of Standards (2011), as well as from the guidance on practice provided by various educational activities and professional statements such as the Association of American Colleges and Universities VALUE Rubrics (2010). Our purpose in this chapter is to examine how this framework informs practice and how that practice, through our various roles as campus educators, reflects our efforts to facilitate moral learning among our students. We explore the learning dynamic between mentor and mentee, including the discomfort, resistance, and retreat that may be an aspect of this learning. We conclude with some ideas for building everyday moral habits that encourage the practice of good mentoring.

The Nature of the Learning Relationship

Effective relationships that can facilitate and sustain the cognitive-structural developmental changes necessary for moral maturity are collaborative in nature. This is a concept explored in Chapter Two. Both learners and mentors must bring certain attitudes, knowledge, and skills to the encounter. The moral coach, or mentor, must "communicate and inspire hope in a student, to maintain belief and pride in the person" (Healy and Liddell, 1998, p. 41). Fundamentally, the learner must bring trust in the relationship—which allows an exploration of and a challenge to assumptions and personal truths that can stifle moral growth. In her discussion of privileged identities, Watt (2007a) suggested that learners must "develop the stamina to sit with discomfort, to continuously seek critical consciousness, and to engage in difficult dialogue" (p. 112). Each of these elements speaks to the awareness, knowledge, and skills necessary to effectively make gains in moral maturity.

Sitting with Discomfort. Consideration of one's moral growth means engaging in conversations about topics that may be uncomfortable for both the learner and the mentor. This discomfort may arise from several sources. Among these may be one's unfamiliarity with the issues involved in the situation; internal moral conflict concerning the issues involved; or unsettling emotions, such as fear, regret, or shame, resulting from examining one's role in the situation. Regardless of the source of the discomfort, learners must practice becoming comfortable with being uncomfortable, and mentors can help them find the perseverance necessary to do so.

It is through discomfort that transformative learning may occur. Developmental theorists have long acknowledged the necessity of challenge to facilitate developmental growth (Sanford, 1966). Differentiation, recognizing the dissonance between one's perspectives and new information being presented, is a prerequisite to the integration that accompanies developmental change (Sanford, 1962) and inevitably brings with it discomfort. As Parker Palmer (1993b) has argued, "an emotionally honest learning space" has the potential to "increase our ability to expose our own ignorance, to ask hard questions, to challenge the validity of what others are saying and receive similar challenges in a spirit of growth" (p. 87).

Seeking Critical Consciousness. Freire (1994) introduced the concept of *critical consciousness* as a vital component of liberation pedagogy. As Watt (2007a) described it, "critical consciousness is the ability to assess and take action against the social, political, and economic elements of oppression in a society" (p. 112). Moral maturity requires this consciousness because morality and ethics are fundamental to advancing community principles of equity, inclusion, and social justice. In essence, critical consciousness is about awareness raising at its root. Therefore, developing an internal moral compass informed by this consciousness requires substantive and broad knowledge about historical patterns and the current roles of power, privilege, and structural inequities in triggering moral issues in campus communities. Exposure to these complex issues may be sufficient for developing a moral sensitivity, recognizing the moral dimensions inherent in tackling social injustices. Therefore, it is of paramount importance that moral learners maintain an openness to continual discovery about self and others and correction of false or incomplete knowledge about social groups, systems, and patterns. Having a companion (or moral coach) help the learner recognize and interpret a situation as problematic is a necessary step in moral growth. This concept is explored in depth in Chapter Two.

Engaging in Difficult Dialogue. Watt (2007a) defined a difficult dialogue as "an exchange of ideas or opinions between citizens within a community that centers on an awakening of potentially conflicting views of beliefs or values about social justice issues" (p. 112). Discussions that lead to moral growth practically demand some level of discomfort and are likely to reveal conflicting points of view and values between the learner and others, including the moral mentor. As such, difficult dialogues of the type described by Watt should be anticipated. Palmer (1993a) asserted that a community embraces conflict and uses it to deepen the educational purpose of educational communities. He goes on to suggest that getting conflicting viewpoints about important issues out in the open is a mark of a healthy community. Appreciating the creative possibilities of conflict and learning how to engage them effectively is an important skill for moral learners to cultivate and practice.

Understanding Resistance and Retreat. In addition to what is required of learners and mentors, understanding resistance is also important to establishing effective moral learning relationships. When difficult dialogues arise around moral and ethical issues, retreat or resistance is a typical response. Mentors are encouraged to check their own discomfort at the door. This retreat and resistance is a common defense mechanism employed to protect one's sense of self (Watt, 2007b).

We offer four strategies for helping learners move through a difficult conversation. First, recognize resistance and retreat to prevent a conversation from spiraling out of control and beyond an effective educational intervention. Second, offer space for emotions and feelings to be identified and expressed. This is consistent with Palmer's (1993b) ideas about allowing for the whole person to be attended to, both intellectually and affectively. Third, use the person's cognitive-structural meaning making to role-model a response that is slightly more complex than the person's initial response. This strategy is commonly advocated by cognitive-structural developmental theorists to promote gains in cognitive complexity (for example, King and Kitchener, 1994). Fourth, seek opportunities for the person to practice using the more cognitively complex and nondefensive response. Also, follow those experiences with reflection and processing to help deepen and solidify the new level of complexity and moral maturity. Through these methods, normal reactions to difficult conversations can be used to spur further moral maturity and strengthen the relationship between learner and moral mentor.

Learning brings with it responsibilities for active engagement. It is particularly important that moral learners build the capacity for handling discomfort, cultivating awareness, and developing the skills necessary to participating in challenging conversations. Nevertheless, this is only half of the learning relationship, and those serving as mentors also have unique responsibilities. We explore the role of the moral mentor next.

Role of the Mentor

The role of a moral mentor is grounded in a relationship with students. In relationships, student affairs educators or faculty members must be willing to "live out loud"—to be authentic, genuine, and evaluative without being viewed as judgmental when discussing dilemmas and decisions. At the same time, they must discern the appropriate boundaries for themselves and the students. They give testimony to the fact that the skills and understanding of moral choices are lifelong and evolving. Next we explore the literature that identifies the characteristics of moral mentors, particularly

Markham's work on the morally serious person (MSP; 2007), Colby and Damon's study of moral exemplars (1992), and an exploration of ethical elders by Liddell, Cooper, Healy, and Stewart (2010).

The Morally Serious Person. Markham (2007) writes from the discipline of theology; however, the intent of his language would be familiar to student affairs professionals. He references the importance of reflection in being a morally serious person and claims that our actions spring from the ethic of care. He differentiates between behavior and thought that is constructive, not destructive, modeling the principle of "do no harm." A morally serious person "creates the disposition that *appreciates* the moment and prepares one to *cope* with the inevitable ambiguity, confusion, and sadness that all lives encounter at certain points and to different degrees of intensity" (p. 182). He goes on to discuss the seven features that distinguish a morally serious person, features that we conclude align well with the beliefs and values of student affairs practice and research.

Responsible citizenship reflects our responsibility to contribute to the community; to support, sustain, and expand the networks of support that define and make communities work. *Intolerance toward discrimination* reflects the need to respect all people and the principle of equality for all. Further, it requires constant reevaluation of our actions and our beliefs to ensure that we continue to examine how we live this feature. *The obligation to be empirically informed* is essential for the MSP to make evidence-based decisions. In the end, this feature permits us to understand the perspective of others. *Disciplined reflection on the cultivation of virtue* reminds us that an MSP must deliberately develop the habits and perspectives to be morally serious. *Consciousness of our sociological conditioning* requires that we understand consciously the culture we live in and understand the importance of the place, language, activities, and other artifacts of that culture. Further, we need to understand that the culture is shaped by the community; in turn, the community creates the context in which we make decisions about how we live and act. *An ordered interior life* reminds us that it is about our thoughts as well as our actions. Thus, it is critical for the MSP to be disciplined in the care of his or her inner life. *Commitment to moral conversation* is a commitment to an examined life through relationship with self and others as a lifelong process. We have an obligation to continuously search for a wide range of perspectives, and this search is developed through conversation.

Although written from the perspective of a theologian, the seven features reflect principles that are familiar to student affairs professionals in their work with students. "The whole concept of the Morally Serious Person is supposed to provide the moral boundaries within which a million different lives could be lived" (Markham, 2007, p. 194).

Moral Exemplars. In Colby and Damon's (1992) study of moral exemplars in various contexts of American life, several characteristics emerged as common. Exemplars demonstrated courage and certainty in the risks and sacrifices they took. Their courage was grounded in their certainty about their moral principles, even when faced with personal hardships. This courage led to an "unhesitating will to act" (p. 70), and exemplars felt little or no sense of loss or suffering about what they had to risk or give up to live up to their principles. A second set of characteristics that emerged for most in the study was their positivity and hopefulness—a belief in the unseen change and the manifestation of their commitments. Exemplars also demonstrated a tendency toward a balance of lasting commitment and sustained capacity for change with self-examination. The self-evaluation and reexamination was evident in many in the study.

For the moral exemplars in their study, moral commitments developed over the span of their lifetimes, with influences coming from those closely connected to the individual. Although they demonstrated an unwavering commitment to core values (frequently identified as honesty, justice, charity, and harmony), they remained open-minded and willing to learn from others, even those with whom they may disagree.

Ethical Elders. In their exploration of the role of ethical elders on campus, Liddell, Cooper, Healy, and Stewart (2010) identify strategies for successful moral mentoring, advising readers to consider these strategies as a continuum of context from the personal to the institutional. To *know yourself* is the first step in being an ethical elder; that is, to be self-aware and to engage in the habit of reflection—and then to help students know themselves. To know others requires that we *seek out and understand others' points of view*. Coaching for growth requires that we take the time to engage in a developmental conversation with students; the outcome is not that the student is compelled by the elder's position but that the student develops a position congruent with his or her knowledge of self. Balancing individual and community needs asks the elder to *consider both the student and the community* in making a decision, taking action, or facilitating the decisions of others, since respecting and valuing the community is as critical as respecting the individual. Finally, ethical elders must *know their institution* and be engaged in it in order to ensure that the climate and culture permit the consideration of ethical issues.

Liddell, Cooper, Healy, and Stewart (2010) go on to claim that "a necessary condition for a learner working through cognitive dissonance is trust—trust that encourages taking risks, sharing perspectives, and reflecting on deeply held beliefs" (p. 13). This trust is cultivated by patience, consistency, kindness, and confidence in the learner. Doing and being what we desire for students is a necessary beginning if we are to serve as moral mentors.

Everyday Habits for Moral Coaching

Although we often talk of models, rubrics, and inspiring ways of thinking about moral mentoring, our impact on students comes in the context of

NEW DIRECTIONS FOR STUDENT SERVICES • DOI: 10.1002/ss

daily life. In this way, it is our everyday habits demonstrated through the example of our behavior that provide guidance to students. In every field of endeavor, there are rules, procedures, and other forms that are learned but that become effective only with practice. In schools and on campuses, we practice fire and emergency drills; we expect that this practice creates a kind of performance memory that will take over in a crisis and guide our actions in reaching safety. Markham (2007) observed, "The irony of a deeply unreflective life is that it is an unappreciated life" (p. 183). Moral habits developed through reflection and internalized through practice become a part of who we are and allow us to achieve moral congruence even when our emotions might otherwise overwhelm us.

Kidder employs the term "Ethical Fitness" in furthering this analogy (1995). In Kidder's explanation, ethical fitness is akin to physical fitness: "You reach it by giving a little effort each day . . . and, without even noticing it you're in shape" and ready for "action" (pp. 58–59). As he points out, to maintain such fitness, you must consistently exercise over time, or your ethical muscles simply lose the strength and the memory necessary to perform vital tasks. As moral mentors, we wish to develop and exercise our own moral habits and model these for our students.

The first stage of such development must be awareness of what values we wish to reflect in our everyday actions and then to constantly reinforce them in practice. Obviously, if we seek to influence wise and ethical choices among our students and colleagues in the face of moral dilemmas—moral challenges that have no clear and absolute answers and that test our value set—we must first understand and practice our own form of moral habit building and the principles on which it is based.

The moral compass is a metaphor for how we understand our moral true north. Based on consciously developed beliefs, values, and principles that we hold personally and professionally, in practice this compass should guide our actions as persons of integrity. Important to the use of a moral compass is Rest's (1986) sense of moral sensitivity and moral judgment: We must be alert to dilemmas and committed to careful judgment as we seek to take the moral course of action. How do we assist our students in doing the same?

The balancing of strengths and weaknesses is a critical part of our daily practice and defines how well we perform as moral actors and mentors. But a balanced response to the moral challenges of our environment, tempering bias with objective knowledge and founded on a core of moral principles, leads to a successful moral development practice. Such development informs us as to when and on what moral basis to take a stand and when or if to alter such stands in order to meet new dilemmas. From this balance come opportunities for continued moral development throughout our life journey.

These are foundational concepts in the journey of a moral mentor. To build on this foundation, we must develop tools and abilities that will aid in moral mentoring with our students. These abilities are sometimes called helping skills, but whatever we call them, they are essential to the intentional practice of the moral mentor. First among these is openness: the ability to perceive the role of the "other" and to have empathy for where that individual stands. It is sharply different from sympathy, which is a more emotional response. It is a conscious effort to maintain an openness of mind without premature judgment. We find empathy, in part, by listening with discernment for the stories of others—without reaching premature judgments or conclusions about the best course of action or, in the case of the moral mentor, without offering guidance before we fully understand the story and moral dilemma before us.

As a mentor, our first obligation is not to offer an answer for the student but to offer the student questions by engaging in thoughtful dialogue and by our own example. It is imperative that we recognize the relevant morally complex dilemmas inherent in choices and decisions. We must be open to the range of possible solutions, the costs or benefits to ourselves and to others, and evaluate possible solutions in light of our moral understanding of these choices. We then choose to act or advise in light of these considerations without regard to our own benefit. Although consequences and our fear of them are reasonable concerns in choosing moral action, we must realize that all actions have consequences and that some, as with moral choices, will be more or less desirable in given situations.

In choosing among alternatives, the moral mentor acknowledges the expectations of others for certain outcomes. We may or may not be able to satisfy these expectations, but our awareness of them is an important component in evaluating the best dilemma resolution. This point leads us to a final moral habit—the ability to "break set," or to judge, which expectations, which rules, do not meet the needs of this dilemma and must therefore be sacrificed in order to reach satisfactory resolution. Kitchener's discussion (1985) of defined moral rules as opposed to the ethical principles of "respecting autonomy, doing no harm, benefiting others and being just" (p. 19) makes this case succinctly: On occasion, specific rules may conflict with one another while principles offer less specificity and a broader range of moral thinking about larger aims. Our choices, our mentoring, are then informed by what Gustafson (1981) has called "informed intuition":

> The final discernment is an informed intuition; it is not the conclusion of a formally logical argument, a strict deduction from a single moral principle, or an absolutely certain result from the exercises of human "reason" alone. There is a final moment of perception that sees the parts in relation to a whole, expresses sensibilities as well as reasoning, and is made in the conditions of human finitude. In complex circumstances, it is not without risk [p. 338].

Everyday moral habits come largely from the foundations, tools, and abilities we discussed. But it is the combination of these into an informed intuition that enables student affairs professionals to be sensitive to moral dilemmas facing themselves and their students. Referring once again to Rest (1986), this sensitivity and judgment lead to the next stages of moral mentoring, motivation, and action. Our willingness to practice those ideals that we espouse, to bring our moral "talk" to actions, is the final distinguishing mark of a moral mentor.

Conclusion

Student affairs professionals have the opportunity to serve as moral mentors for their students. Doing this requires that we understand that one of the fundamental purposes in a college education is for students to find their purpose in life. We argue that perhaps our most sacred duty is to engage in the meaning-making process with students. When called to guide students in this important quest, we are asked to show up with authenticity with students, because the process of discovering purpose comes in the relationship between the mentor and the student. These noble principles need to be lived every day.

References

American College Personnel Association and National Association of Student Personnel Administrators. "Professional Competency Areas for Student Affairs Practitioners," 2010. Retrieved June 20, 2012, from http://www2.myacpa.org/au/governance/Joint_Task_Force_of_Professional_Competencies.php.

Association of American Colleges and Universities. "VALUE: Valid Assessment of learning in Undergraduate Education," 2010. Retrieved June 20, 2012, from http://www.aacu.org/value/rubrics/index.cfm?CFID=36234342&CFTOKEN=89047459.

Astin, A. W., Asin, H. S., and Lindholm, J. A. Cultivating the Spirit: How College Can Enhance Students' Inner Lives. San Francisco: Jossey-Bass, 2010.

Colby, A., and Damon, W. Some Do Care: Contemporary Lives of Moral Commitment. New York: Free Press, 1992.

Council for the Advancement of Standards. "Standards," 2011. Retrieved June 21, 2012, from http://www.cas.edu/.

Freire, P. Pedagogy of the Oppressed, 20th anniversary ed. Translated by Myra Bergman Ramos. New York: Continuum, 1994.

Gustafson, J. M. Ethics from a Theocentric Perspective. Chicago: University of Chicago Press, 1981.

Healy, M. A., and Liddell, D. L. "The Developmental Conversation: Facilitating Moral and Intellectual Growth in Our Students." In D. L. Cooper and J. Lancaster (eds.), Beyond Law and Policy: Reaffirming the Role of Student Affairs. New Directions for Student Services, no. 82. San Francisco: Jossey-Bass, 1998.

Kidder, R. M. How Good People Make Tough Choices: Resolving the Dilemmas of Ethical Living. New York: Fireside Press, 1995.

King, P. M., and Kitchener, K. S. Developing Reflective Judgment: Understanding and Promoting Intellectual Growth and Critical Thinking in Adolescents and Adults. San Francisco: Jossey-Bass, 1994.

Kitchener, K. S. "Ethical Principles and Ethical Decisions in Student Affairs." In H. J. Canon and R. D. Brown (eds.), *Applied Ethics in Student Services.* New Directions in Student Services, no. 30. San Francisco: Jossey-Bass, 1985.

Liddell, D. L., Cooper, D. L., Healy, M. A. and Stewart, D. L. "Ethical Elders: Campus Role Models for Moral Development," *About Campus*, 2010, *15*(1), 11–17.

Markham, I. S. *Do Morals Matter: A Guide to Contemporary Religious Ethics.* Malden, Mass.: Blackwell, 2007.

National Association of Scholars. "Rebuilding CAMPUS Community: The wrong Imperative," 2008. Retrieved June 21, 2012, from http://www.nas.org/polArticles.cfm?Doc_Id=251.

Palmer, P. J. "Community, Conflict, and Ways of Knowing." Center for Courage and Renewal, 1993a. Retrieved January 15, 2012, from http://www.couragerenewal.org/parker/writings/community-conflict.

Palmer, P. J. *To Know as We Are Known: Education as a Spiritual Journey.* San Francisco: Harper Collins, 1993b.

Rest, J. *Moral Development: Advances in Research and Theory.* New York: Praeger, 1986.

Sanford, N. "Developmental Status of the Entering Freshmen." In N. Sanford (ed.), *The American College Student.* New York: John Wiley & Sons, 1962.

Sanford, N. *Self and Society: Social Change and Individual Development.* New York: Atherton Press, 1966.

Watt, S. K. "Editor's Notes." *College Student Affairs Journal*, 2007a, *26*(2), 112–113.

Watt, S. K. "Difficult Dialogues, Privilege and Social Justice: Uses of the Privileged Identity Exploration (PIE) Model in Student Affairs Practice." *College Student Affairs Journal*, 2007b, *26*(2), 114–126.

MARGARET A. HEALY *is a professor of educational leadership at the University of North Dakota.*

JAMES M. LANCASTER *is a professor of human development and psychological counseling at Appalachian State University.*

DEBORA L. LIDDELL *is an associate professor and program coordinator of the Higher Education and Student Affairs Graduate Program at the University of Iowa.*

DAFINA LAZARUS STEWART *is an associate professor of higher education and student affairs at Bowling Green State University.*

9

In this era of increased accountability, it is important to consider how student affairs researches and assesses the outcomes of our efforts to increase moral competence. This chapter examines both qualitative and quantitative inquiry methods for measuring moral development.

Providing Evidence in the Moral Domain

Diane L. Cooper, Debora L. Liddell, Tiffany J. Davis, Kira Pasquesi

The pressure on higher education to provide evidence for our work means that we need to assess our efforts to help students grow and develop. The first step in approaching your assessment, then, is to clarify your intended targets. Do you want to measure moral reasoning or sensitivity? Are you more interested in empathy and concern for others or a commitment to social justice? In this chapter, we review the instrumentation and methods typically used to measure moral competence, and suggest close proxies for the domain.

Measuring the Moral Domain Through Quantitative Methods

Most of the widely used measures of moral growth utilizing quantitative methodology discussed here are based in Kohlberg's work (1981) on moral education and reasoning.

Defining Issues Test. The Defining Issues Test (DIT) is a well-known and well-respected measure of moral reasoning across many academic disciplines for over thirty-five years. Few professionals are unfamiliar with the famous Heinz dilemma that appeared in Rest's (1979) original version of the instrument. The Defining Issues Test, Version 2 (DIT-2), updates the original dilemmas and issue statements, is shorter, and has clearer instructions (Rest, Narvaez, Thoma, and Bebeau, 1999). The DIT-2 emphasizes cognition, promotes self-construction, portrays development, and characterizes the shift to postconventional moral thinking. Whereas Kohlberg's theory outlines six stages, the DIT uses schemas that may shift across traditional Kohlbergian stages. These schemas are classified as: Personal Interest, Maintaining Norms, and Postconventional (Rest, Narvaez, Thoma, and Bebeau, 1999). The DIT-2 consists of five dilemmas designed to elicit the evaluation of conflicting values (for example, truth versus privacy). After

NEW DIRECTIONS FOR STUDENT SERVICES, no. 139, Fall 2012 © Wiley Periodicals, Inc.
Published online in Wiley Online Library (wileyonlinelibrary.com) • DOI: 10.1002/ss.20026

reading each dilemma, test takers are asked to complete three different tasks.

1. Select the action the character would take from three available options.
2. Rate the twelve issues statements that follow each dilemma in terms of their moral importance based on the test taker's own moral schemas.
3. Select four of the issue statements and rank them based on their level of importance (Maeda, Thoma, and Bebeau, 2009; Rest, Narvaez, Thoma, and Bebeau, 1999).

The DIT-2 generates an N2 score—that is the New Index Score—resulting from a different scoring method from the original DIT. The N2 score references the extent to which postconventional items are favored over other schemas. The N2 has been standardized and adjusted so that it is on the same scale as the original DIT P (postconventional schema) index scores and has been shown to outperform the P index scores on construct validity (Bebeau and Thoma, 2003).

The DIT-2 is not without its limitations and critiques. The fixed dilemmas not only make pre- and posttesting of educational interventions a challenge (as students may remember the dilemmas), but topics of dilemmas may not be associated with or relevant to the student demographic or discipline in which the researchers might be interested (Shawver and Sennetti, 2009). In addition, the DIT has been shown to be subject to various biases, including gender, religious, and discipline (Shawver and Sennetti, 2009).

Implications for Student Affairs. Among the advantages of using the DIT-2, the structured nature of the test, its ability to be self-administered, and the objective scoring (Shawver and Sennetti, 2009) seem to be of most benefit. As student affairs professionals consider the use of the DIT-2 in their practice, it is also important to remember the goal of the DIT versions has been to understand how people think about social problems (Rizzo and Swisher, 2004). Thus, the DIT focuses on the macromorality—issues embedded in rules, role systems, and formal institutions (Rest, Narvaez, Thoma, and Bebeau, 1999; Rizzo and Swisher, 2004). If the goal of your research is to look at micromorality—everyday ethics that focus on the particular, face-to-face relationships with people—an alternative approach to measure moral reasoning might be appropriate.

Moral Judgment Interview. An interview protocol in a positivist tradition is the Moral Judgment Interview (MJI), a measure of moral reasoning based in the work of Kohlberg (1959). The MJI uses an interview method that seeks to identify the reasons *why* participants perceive certain actions as morally just or preferred to then determine participants' stage of reasoning according to the six-stage model of moral development as outlined by Kohlberg. The initial procedure for administering the MJI involved participants being interviewed after they were presented with a series of situations involving moral conflicts (Elm and Weber, 1994). After the dilemma is presented, the participant is asked a series of open-ended, probing questions by the researcher to elicit information regarding how the participant would resolve the dilemma (Rest, Narvaez, Thoma, and Bebeau, 1999). The questions elicit judgments about what one *should* do to resolve to the dilemma rather than what one *would* do in the given situation (Elm and Weber, 1994).

The scoring for the MJI has been refined over the years (Colby and others, 1983; Rest, Narvaez, Thoma, and Bebeau, 1999) to increase reliability and validity of the interview data scores.

Konstanz Method of Moral Dilemma Discussion and Moral Judgment Test. The method of moral dilemma discussion in the development of moral competence was first suggested by Blatt and Kohlberg (1975) for use in children's classrooms and has been shown to be highly effective across various age groups, from ten-year-olds to adults (Lind, 2006). As with some other measures of moral judgment, the assessment method may also coax moral growth. This teaching method rests on key assumptions proffered by Kohlberg (1984): in a democratic society, it is important that individuals not only hold high moral values, but they must also possess the ability to apply them in everyday situations and the competence to make judgments that are aligned with their values (Lind, 2005).

The Konstanz Method of Dilemma Discussion (KMDD) uses dilemmas that do not put the test taker into the story but expose the conflict between the individual's moral beliefs and the content of the dilemma (Lind, 2006). Designed to evoke moral emotion to stimulate learning, the KMDD can promote reflection and dialogue through deep group discussion. This is primarily achieved through small-group sessions within a class (Lind, 2006).

Lind developed a new measure of moral judgment competence, the Moral Judgment Test (MJT). The MJT is a competence test that provides a measure of judgment behavior based on two aspects: moral judgment competence as described by Kohlberg (1959) and moral orientations or preferences (Lind, 2006). The standard version of the MJT consists of two dilemmas in which individuals are asked to judge the acceptability of arguments both pro and con for the decisions made by the protagonist in the dilemmas.

Implications for Student Affairs. The effectiveness of the Konstanz method supports the argument that moral competencies can be taught. However, "this 'teaching' must be different from traditional instruction and classroom management. It must be open and democratic and it must focus on creating a trustable and supportive learning environment" (Lind, 2006, p. 194). Student affairs has and will continue to contribute to this holistic learning process by intentionally designing such environments where students can learn through action, contemplation, reflection, and emotional engagement (National Association of Student Personnel Administrators and American College Personnel Association, 2004)—environments that can best foster moral competence and development. Programs and initiatives such as living-learning communities, service-learning programs, and leadership experiences represent ripe learning environments in which to explore students' moral competence and orientations. And although the Konstanz method has been deemed reliable and valid for use with college populations (Lind, 2006), it has not been widely used as a research or assessment measure within student affairs and may be impractical to do so. It requires time and training to construct environments to facilitate deep and critical discussion of complex moral issues. However, as student affairs professionals partner with faculty to integrate co-curricular experiences with classroom academic credit, the use of moral dilemma discussion and/or the MJT might be feasible.

Measure of Moral Orientation. Liddell's Measure of Moral Orientation (MMO) (Liddell, 2006; Liddell, Halpin, and Halpin, 1992) is an instrument designed to measure an individual's moral orientation as either care or justice oriented, as stressed by Gilligan and Kohlberg, respectively (Hight, 2004; Kuyel and Glover, 2010). Whereas the DIT measures moral judgment, the stage of moral reasoning a person exhibits in thinking about a dilemma, the MMO measures the extent to which students prefer care or justice orientations in decision making, tapping into Rest's moral sensitivity component.

The revised MMO-2 is a dilemma-based, fifty-two-item self-report instrument. Students are first introduced to seven moral dilemmas that represent situations most likely to be encountered by traditional-age college students. They are asked to imagine themselves as the protagonist in the dilemma and then to agree or disagree with the fifty-two response items that correspond to the dilemmas. Two scores are generated: a care score and a justice score. The higher the individual score on a scale, the greater orientation to the construct being measured. In the original instrument, a validation self-description scale was included. The self-description scores were highly correlated with the care and justice scores; therefore, they were dropped in the revised version (Liddell, Halpin, and Halpin, 1992; Liddell, 2006). The Testing Manual (Liddell, 2006), available from the author, may be helpful to users.

Implications for Practice. Student affairs, in many regards, is an interdisciplinary profession. Thus, many of the instruments and measures of moral development that we use in our research have not been intended for college students. Liddell's MMO (Liddell, Halpin, and Halpin, 1992) was developed specifically with the college context in mind. The dilemmas and responses were cultivated from discussions with undergraduate students, which represents a strength of this instrument. However, there are few published articles utilizing the MMO (Hight, 2004; Liddell, 1998; Kuyel and Glover, 2010). Future research studies could explore moral growth using this instrument as it has been shown to be both reliable and valid (Liddell and Davis, 1996; Jaffee and Hyde, 2000; Kuyel and Glover, 2010).

Although this is not an exhaustive list of the quantitative approaches to measuring moral development, it does review the more commonly used instruments. A central strength in using quantitative methods lies in the established reliability and validity of these instruments over time and across various studies. For further information on these data, please refer to the source citations provided at the close of this chapter.

Qualitative Methods to Assess Moral Issues

Several appropriate qualitative methods used to assess various dimensions of moral growth, moral orientation, or moral reasoning are reviewed next.

Interviews. The most popular qualitative approach to assessment of the moral domain is the interview. An open-ended interview has the advantage of being fluid so that the interviewer may pursue a trajectory of reason, allowing the researcher and the interviewee to jointly construct meaning. The most common interview protocol is traced back to Nona Lyons (1988). Following the assertions of Carol Gilligan, Lyons crafted a protocol that allowed for the study of self-definition and moral judgment about real-life moral dilemmas. Like Gilligan (1977), Lyons found that the construction and resolution of moral dilemmas was related to how one saw oneself in the world—as either a connected or a separate person. Connectedness, she found, was closely related to using an ethic of care, while seeing oneself as separate from others was closely related to using an ethic of justice. Participants were asked to describe themselves, to identify a situation or incident that might be considered a moral dilemma. They were probed about what made it a moral conflict and what options for resolving the conflict were considered. Responses were coded as per Lyons's coding scheme (1988). The protocol was replicated in a study by Liddell (1998), which examined the relationship of moral orientation (care–justice), self-description (connected–separate), and scores on the MMO.

In a study of care reasoning in real-life moral conflicts, Juujärvi (2006) used Eva Skoe's Ethic of Care Interview (ECI; 1993). The ECI uses a participant-generated real-life problem and three interpersonal dilemmas that centered on crisis pregnancy, marital infidelity, and caring for an aging parent. The ECI measures Gilligan's ethic of care and calculates a score on the Gilligan theoretical continuum. Skoe provides researchers an interview manual to follow.

Sadler (2004) used interviews about genetic engineering dilemmas with college students to measure moral sensitivity. The dilemmas in the interview were about using embryonic tissue to affect Huntington's disease and cloning as a reproductive option. Follow-up interviews allowed participants to explore the rationale behind their decisions.

NEW DIRECTIONS FOR STUDENT SERVICES • DOI: 10.1002/ss

Finally, Ochoa (2008) used interviews to investigate character development of master's students through the mentoring process in a student affairs division. In this study, participants were asked to describe personal character traits that were important, identify how those traits were developed, and explain how the mentoring relationship developed in a way to affect the development of character. The data were analyzed using coding based on hermeneutic phenomenology theory. This protocol would be useful to those looking at the role of mentors and role models on campus.

Case Studies. Mathiasen (2000) employed a case study approach to study moral development in fraternity members. He examined documents, conducted interviews, and made observations of members of a fraternity to identify the sources of positive influence of morality. This study serves as a good example of how to study moral development using a case study approach.

Multimethod Approaches. Several researchers have used a multimethod approach to assessing moral development. For example, Liddell (1998, 2000) compared responses on the MMO with semistructured interviews with students. The interviews included exploration of at least one dilemma on the MMO and a discussion of self-generated dilemmas, which were coded and analyzed for themes. Dilemma topics generated by students included conflicts with friends, breaking away from parents, dealing with loss, responding to crisis pregnancy, confronting racism, and breaking the law.

Controlling for confounding variables, such as environmental influence, course or instructor differences, or cognitive ability, complicates the true measure of impact of our initiatives. King and Mayhew (2002) suggest the use of case studies and ethnographies to study institutional characteristics and student cultures and subcultures. Understanding what retards moral growth may be even more important than understanding what contributes to it.

Proxies for Moral Competence

In their review of the literature about moral judgment (as measured by the DIT), King and Mayhew (2002) conclude that there are shared relationships between moral competence and other areas of development. These useful proxies, or close approximations, to moral development may also be worth pursuing: attitudes about religion and spirituality, social issues, tolerance and diversity, and perspective taking. Bringle, Phillips, and Hudson (2010) provide an excellent resource for identifying measures of various constructs related to participation in service learning that can be extended to other activities identified in this text for promoting moral growth.

New Directions for Student Services • DOI: 10.1002/ss

Assessing Organizational and Programmatic Outcomes

The instruments presented in this chapter are designed primarily to be used with individual students to explore research-related questions. However, as Boyd and Brackmann pointed out in Chapter Four, there are times when assessment activities must be conducted at the institutional level to assess the extent that programs are contributing to the moral growth of students.

Measuring changes in moral development and decision making at the organization or programmatic level is challenging for a number of reasons. One difficulty of particular interest in this discussion is that few administrative units have learning outcomes related to moral change that can be attributed to activities within their unit. It was argued earlier in this text that perhaps student affairs divisions should have meaningful discussions about creating purposeful activities that will be directed toward increased moral reasoning, civility, and citizenship.

Student affairs departments or units can use the Council for the Advancement of Standards in Higher Education (CAS; 2009) Learning and Developmental Outcomes (LDOs) as a starting point for creating learning outcomes that can guide practice toward a more integrated approach to facilitating moral growth. The LDOs were developed through a CAS think tank that included both CAS board members and writers of *Learning Reconsidered 2* (American College Personnel Association and others, 2006): "To comply with CAS standards, institutional programs and services must identify relevant and desirable learning from these domains, assess relevant and desirable learning, and articulate how their programs and services contribute to domains not specifically assessed. For each of the domains, CAS offers examples illustrating achievement of the student learning outcomes" (CAS, 2011, paragraph 2).

One domain, Humanitarian and Civic Engagement, outlines specific learning outcomes that can be used by professional staff to modify current mission, goals, and objectives in light of the suggestions offered in this text. Examples of possible learning outcomes include "consideration of the welfare of others in decision-making; engages in critical reflection and principled dissent; understands and participates in relevant governance systems; educates and facilitates the civic engagement of others" (CAS, 2009, p. 3).

The Student Affairs Division at the University of Georgia has incorporated this concept into its overall strategic plan for enhancing student learning through the inclusion of the Student Affairs Learning and Development Outcomes (SALDOs). The SALDOs were collaboratively created by members of the division, the Office of Student Affairs Assessment, student affairs faculty members, and doctoral students reviewing the CAS *Frameworks for Assessing Learning and Development Outcomes* (Strayhorn, 2006), *Learning Reconsidered* (Keeling, 2004), and *Powerful Partnerships* (American Association for Higher Education, American College Personnel Association, and National Association of Student Personnel Administrators,

1998). "The SALDOs are intended to be a framework or map of the Division's collective values from which more specific outcomes are developed and assessed" (Atchley, 2008, p. 1). Eight domains were identified, including social responsibility, which involves understanding the importance of service to others; awareness of community needs; view of self as a member of the global community; participation in development, maintenance, and/or orderly change of community, social, and legal standards or norms; and tolerance and care for others. Functional units then use the SALDOs to review and assess their own programs and practices related to each domain.

Challenges in Measurement

Despite our best efforts to assess moral development, there remain challenging issues, including dilemma type, interrater reliability, and the role of the researcher in interview studies. The Heinz dilemma has provided the common stimulus for many measures of moral development; in this dilemma, a man whose wife is dying of cancer must decide whether to steal an overpriced drug that will save her life. However, many researchers have studied the effect that a hypothetical dilemma, such as the Heinz story, may have on people's reasoning. Wark and Krebs (1996) found that the type of dilemma affected not only the level of moral reasoning but also the moral orientation (care or justice) evoked in response to the dilemma. Impersonal dilemmas, such as capital punishment, pulled for more justice responses, while personal dilemmas, such as responding to temptation, were more likely to evoke discussion about threats to relationship (a care-oriented response). Professionals interested in measuring moral development should take care that their discussion stimulus cultivates a genuine opportunity to explore moral issues to which students can relate.

Finally, the role of the interviewer may present a thorny issue in the assessment of cognitive and moral development. Baxter Magolda (2004), following her sixteen-year study of young adults, reflected on her partnership with participants and the privilege of being not just a spectator but a cotraveler on their journeys. Likewise, Liddell (1998) reflected on her role as an interviewer of college students about their moral choices. The opportunity to co-construct meaning with students is a powerful event for both learner and interviewer. Interviewing students about their moral conflict requires acknowledging the difficulty in separating oneself from what one is actually hearing and seeing. There is nothing objective about being in this role and approaching assessment this way. Just by asking the questions ("Can you describe a moral or ethical conflict you've had recently? What made this difficult for you? How did you resolve it? Do you think you made the right decision? Why?"), we situate ourselves as prompters for growth. We are no longer bearing witness, we are—by our questions—

prompting students' development as they work through their conflict in front of us. Baxter Magolda's participants confirmed this: "Participants told me that reflecting on their experience in the interviews changed their thinking about it and made them more aware of it in the [coming] year" (2004, p. 36).

Trow (1976) argued that the question is not "whether" higher education contributes to the moral development of students but "how" this development unfolds. Assessing and evaluating students engaged in various co-curricular programs and activities are our best ways of understanding this process. In this chapter, we have presented both quantitative and qualitative approaches to the measurement of moral development and growth. Regardless of the measurement target, we encourage researchers to clarify their criteria before beginning assessment of their outcomes. In times of decreasing resources amid increasing calls for public accountability, we need to continue to enhance our ability to show campus decision makers the impact student affairs activities have on student moral growth.

References

American Association for Higher Education, American College Personnel Association, and National Association of Student Personnel Administrators. *Powerful Partnerships: A Shared Responsibility for Learning*. Washington, D.C.: National Association of Student Personnel Administrators, 1998.

American College Personnel Association and others. *Learning Reconsidered 2: A Practical Guide to Implementing a Campus-wide Focus on the Student Experience*. Washington, D.C.: National Association of Student Personnel Administrators, 2006.

Atchley, L. "The Student Affairs Learning and Development Objectives (SALDOs) Initiative." *Student Pulse*, 2008, 2(1), 1–2.

Baxter Magolda, M. "Evolution of a Constructivist Conceptualization of Epistemological Reflection." *Educational Psychologist*, 2004, 39(1), 31–42.

Bebeau, M. J., and Thoma, S. J. *Guide for DIT-2: A Guide for Using the Defining Issues Test, Version 2 (DIT-2) and the Scoring Service of the Center for the Study of Ethical Development*. Minneapolis: Center for the Study of Ethical Development, 2003.

Blatt, M., and Kohlberg, L. "The Effect of Classroom Moral Discussion Upon Children's Level of Moral Judgment." *Journal of Moral Education*, 1975, 4, 129–161.

Bringle, R. G., Phillips, M, A., and Hudson, M. *The Measure of Service Learning: Research Scales to Assess Student Experiences*. Washington, D.C.: American Psychological Association, 2010.

Colby, A., Kohlberg, L., Gibbs, J., Lieberman, M., Fischer, K., and Saltzstein, H. D. "A Longitudinal Study of Moral Judgment." *Monographs of the Society for Research in Child Development*, 1983, 48(1/2), 1–124.

Council for the Advancement of Standards in Higher Education. *CAS Professional Standards for Higher Education*, 7th ed. Washington, D.C.: Council for the Advancement of Standards in Higher Education, 2009.

Council for the Advancement of Standards in Higher Education. "Learning and Development Outcomes." Accessed December 23, 2011, from http://www.cas.edu/index. php/learning-and-developental-outcomes/.

Elm, D. R., and Weber, J. "Measuring Moral Judgment: The Moral Judgment Interview or the Defining Issues Test?" *Journal of Business Ethics*, 1994, 13, 341–355.

Gilligan, C. "In a Different Voice: Women's Conception of Self and Morality." *Harvard Educational Review*, 1977, 47, 481–517.

Hight, D. L. "Context, Moral Orientation and Self-Esteem: Impacting the Moral Development of College Students." Unpublished doctoral dissertation. College of Education, University of Georgia, 2004.

Jaffee, S., and Hyde, J. S. "Gender Difference in Moral Orientation: A Meta-Analysis." *Psychological Bulletin*, 2000, 126(5), 703–726.

Juujärvi, S. "Care Reasoning in Real-Life Moral Conflicts." *Journal of Moral Education*, 2006, 35(2), 197–211.

Keeling, R. P. (ed.). *Learning Reconsidered: A Campus-wide Focus on the Student Experience*. Washington, D.C.: National Association of Student Personnel Administrators and the American College Personnel Association, 2004.

King, P. M., and Mayhew, M. J. "Moral Judgment Development in Higher Education: Insights from the Defining Issues Test." *Journal of Moral Education*, 2002, 31(3), 247–270.

Kohlberg, L. "The Development of Modes of Thinking and Choices in Years 10 to 16." Unpublished doctoral dissertation. University of Chicago, 1959.

Kohlberg, L. *Essays in Moral Development: The Philosophy of Moral Development (Vol. 1)*. New York: Harper & Row, 1981.

Kuyel, N., and Glover, R. J. "Moral Reasoning and Moral Orientation of U.S. and Turkish University Students." *Psychological Reports*, 2010, 107(2), 463–479.

Liddell, D. L. "Comparison of Semistructured Interviews with a Quantitative Measure of Moral Orientation." *Journal of College Student Development*, 1998, 39, 169–178.

Liddell, D. L. "In Their Words: Analysis of Real-Life Dilemmas vs. Hypothetical Dilemmas and Their Relationship to Moral Orientation." Paper presented at the Association of Moral Education meeting, Glasgow, Scotland, November 2000.

Liddell, D. L. *The Measure of Moral Orientation: A Testing Manual*. Iowa City: University of Iowa, 2006.

Liddell, D. L., and Davis, T. "The Measure of Moral Orientation: Reliability and Validity Evidence." *Journal of College Student Development*, 1996, 37, 485–493.

Liddell, D. L., Halpin, G., and Halpin, W. G. "The Measure of Moral Orientation: Measuring the Ethics of Care and Justice." *Journal of College Student Development*, 1992, 33(4), 325–330.

Lind, G. "Moral Dilemma Discussion-Revisited: The Konstanz Method." *Europe's Journal of Psychology*, 2005, 1(1). Retrieved August 12, 2011, from www.ejop.org.

Lind, G. "Effective Moral Education: The Konstanz Method of Dilemma Discussion." *Hellenic Journal of Psychology*, 2006, 3, 189–196.

Lyons, N. P. "Two Perspectives: On Self, Relationships, and Morality." In C. Gilligan, J. Ward, & J. Taylor (eds.), *Mapping the Moral Domain*. Cambridge, Mass.: Harvard University Press, 1988.

Maeda, Y., Thoma, S. J., and Bebeau, M. J. "Understanding the Relationship Between Moral Judgment Development and Individual Characteristics: The Role of Educational Contexts." *Journal of Educational Psychology*, 2009, 101(1), 233–247.

Mathiasen, R. E. "Moral Development in Fraternity Members: A Case Study." Unpublished doctoral dissertation. University of Nebraska, December 2000.

National Association of Student Personnel Administrators and American College Personnel Association. *Learning Reconsidered: A Campus-wide Focus on the Student Experience*. Washington, D.C.: National Association of Student Personnel Administrators and American College Personnel Association, 2004.

Ochoa, G. S. "Perceived Character Development in a Mentoring Relationship from the Voices of Students and Their Student Affairs Mentors." Unpublished doctoral dissertation. Duquesne University, August 2008.

Rest, J. R. *Development in Judging Moral Issues*. Minneapolis, Minnesota: University of Minnesota Press, 1979.

Rest, J. R., Narvaez, D., Thoma, S., and Bebeau, M. J. "DIT2: Devising and Testing a Revised Instrument of Moral Judgment." *Journal of Educational Psychology*, 1999, *91*(4), 644–659.

Rizzo, A.-M., and Swisher, L. L. "Comparing the Stewart-Sprinthall Management Survey and the Defining Issues Test-2 as Measures of Moral Reasoning in Public Administration." *Journal of Public Administration Research and Theory*, 2004, *14*(3), 335–348.

Sadler, T. D. "Moral Sensitivity and Its Contribution to the Resolution of Socio-Scientific Issues." *Journal of Moral Education*, 2004, *33*(3), 339–358.

Shawver, T. J., and Sennetti, J. T. "Measuring Ethical Sensitivity and Evaluation." *Journal of Business Ethics*, 2009, *88*, 663–678.

Skoe, E. E. *The Ethic of Care Interview Manual*. Oslo: University of Oslo, 1993.

Strayhorn, T. L. *Frameworks for Assessing Learning and Development Outcomes*. Washington, D.C.: Council for the Advancement of Standards in Higher Education, 2006.

Trow, M. "Higher Education and Moral Development." *AAUP Bulletin*, 1976, *62*(1), 20–27.

Wark, G. R., and Krebs, D. L. "Gender and Dilemma Differences in Real-Life Moral Judgment." *Developmental Psychology*, 1996, *32*(2), 220–230.

DIANE L. COOPER *is a professor of college student affairs administration at the University of Georgia.*

DEBORA L. LIDDELL *is an associate professor and program coordinator of the Higher Education and Student Affairs Program at the University of Iowa.*

TIFFANY J. DAVIS *is a doctoral candidate in College Student Affairs Administration at the University of Georgia.*

KIRA PASQUESI *is a second-year doctoral student in the Higher Education and Student Affairs Program at the University of Iowa.*

INDEX

Page references followed by *t* indicate a table.

ORDER FORM
SUBSCRIPTION AND SINGLE ISSUES

DISCOUNTED BACK ISSUES:

Use this form to receive 20% off all back issues of *New Directions for Student Services*.
All single issues priced at **$23.20** (normally $29.00)

TITLE	ISSUE NO.	ISBN
_____	_____	_____
_____	_____	_____
_____	_____	_____

Call 888-378-2537 or see mailing instructions below. When calling, mention the promotional code JBNND to receive your discount. For a complete list of issues, please visit www.josseybass.com/go/ndss

SUBSCRIPTIONS: (1 YEAR, 4 ISSUES)

☐ New Order   ☐ Renewal

U.S.	☐ Individual: $89	☐ Institutional: $275
CANADA/MEXICO	☐ Individual: $89	☐ Institutional: $315
ALL OTHERS	☐ Individual: $113	☐ Institutional: $349

Call 888-378-2537 or see mailing and pricing instructions below.
Online subscriptions are available at www.onlinelibrary.wiley.com

ORDER TOTALS:

Issue / Subscription Amount: $ _____

Shipping Amount: $ _____
(for single issues only – subscription prices include shipping)

Total Amount: $ _____

SHIPPING CHARGES:

| First Item | $6.00 |
| Each Add'l Item | $2.00 |

(No sales tax for U.S. subscriptions. Canadian residents, add GST for subscription orders. Individual rate subscriptions must be paid by personal check or credit card. Individual rate subscriptions may not be resold as library copies.)

BILLING & SHIPPING INFORMATION:

☐ **PAYMENT ENCLOSED:** *(U.S. check or money order only. All payments must be in U.S. dollars.)*

☐ **CREDIT CARD:**   ☐ VISA   ☐ MC   ☐ AMEX

Card number _____ Exp. Date _____

Card Holder Name _____ Card Issue # _____

Signature _____ Day Phone _____

☐ **BILL ME:** *(U.S. institutional orders only. Purchase order required.)*

Purchase order # _____
Federal Tax ID 13559302 • GST 89102-8052

Name _____

Address _____

Phone _____ E-mail _____

Copy or detach page and send to: **John Wiley & Sons, One Montgomery Street, Suite 1200, San Francisco, CA 94104-4594**

Order Form can also be faxed to: **888-481-2665**

PROMO JBNND